CHARCUTERIE
boards

CHARCUTERIE
boards

**PLATTERS,
BOARDS, PLATES
& SIMPLE RECIPES
TO SHARE**

**Miranda Ballard
& Louise Pickford**

with photography by Ian Wallace

rps

RYLAND PETERS & SMALL
LONDON • NEW YORK

Senior Designer Toni Kay
Editor Kate Reeves-Brown
Head of Production
   Patricia Harrington
Creative Director
   Leslie Harrington
Editorial Director Julia Charles

Food Stylists Louise Pickford
   & Lucy McKelvie
Prop Stylists Louise Pickford
   & Steve Painter
Indexer Hilary Bird

First published in 2023 by
Ryland Peters & Small
20–21 Jockey's Fields
London WC1R 4BW
and
341 E 116th Street
New York, 10029
www.rylandpeters.com

Please note that recipes by
Miranda Ballard included in this
book were previously published by
Ryland Peters & Small in her book
entitled *Charcuterie* (2014)

www.rylandpeters.com

10 9 8 7 6 5 4 3 2 1

Text © Miranda Ballard 2014,
2023, with the exception of text
on pages 10–53, 57 (top) and 64
© Louise Pickford 2023
Design and photography ©
Ryland Peters & Small 2014, 2023
See page 176 for full image credits.

Printed in China

ISBN: 978-1-78879-515-9

A CIP record for this book is
available from the British Library.
US Library of Congress CIP data
has been applied for.

NOTES
• All spoon measurements are
level unless otherwise specified.
• All eggs are medium (UK) or large
(US), unless otherwise specified.
Uncooked or partially cooked eggs
should not be served to the very
old, frail, young children, pregnant
women or those with compromised
immune systems.
• Fruit and vegetables are medium-
sized, unless otherwise stated.
• Chillies/chiles are fresh, unless
otherwise stated.
• When a recipe calls for the
grated zest of citrus fruit, buy
unwaxed fruit and wash well before
using. If you can only find treated
fruit, scrub well in warm soapy
water before using.

• To sterilize preserving jars, wash
them in hot, soapy water and rinse
in boiling water. Place in a large
saucepan and cover with hot water.
With the saucepan lid on, bring the
water to a boil and continue boiling
for 15 minutes. Turn off the heat
and leave the jars in the hot water
until just before they are to be filled.
Invert the jars onto a clean dish
towel to dry. Sterilize the lids for
5 minutes, by boiling or according
to the manufacturer's instructions.
Jars should be filled and sealed
while they are still hot.

FOOD SAFETY
• The information in this book is
based on the authors' experiences.
Guidelines for safety are included
within recipes, and these should
be followed. Neither the authors
nor the publisher can be held
responsible for any harm or injury
that arises from the application
of ideas in this book.
• Uncooked or partially cooked
meats should not be served to
the very old, frail, young children,
pregnant women or those with
compromised immune systems.

CONTENTS

Introduction

Will you allow me to start with an assumption? If you bought this book, or someone thought this book might be a good gift for you, then I think we already agree about how to source our meat. I think that we're the ones upholding our side of the deal, the deal between humans and livestock. That, as the term 'animal husbandry' reminds us, we are part of a binding contract that relies on our respect for animals and their welfare.

I think we're the ones who appreciate that there are challenges involved in finding where this contract is commercially viable, but we have taken the time to learn where that balance lies. We're proud to understand the difference between 'clean' meat and cheap meat.

I think you'll already anticipate that whenever I refer to 'farming', I mean 'good farming'; when I talk about 'meat', I mean 'good meat'; and when I cover the wonderful range of products under the heading of 'charcuterie and salumi', it's understood that the entire process of the procurement and production of these products should uphold the contract between humans and livestock.

So I'm not going to talk about how to find and afford these products, because I know you're already with me on this. I'm sure that you share the same enjoyment and confidence from making a recipe with good meat and knowing that it will deliver on taste.

I'll just carry on then – and I really hope you enjoy the ideas and recipes in this book!

Three reasons why I love charcuterie

The first reason is that it's a gift to home cooking – it's a gift of expertise, passion and time. These products can sometimes take longer to produce than the time it takes to build a skyscraper (jamón Ibérico springs to mind – see page 20). When you think

about the processes involved, you realise how much effort goes into the products that you can buy pretty conveniently and affordably nowadays. The process starts in the same way as it does for raw meat. Let's take a quick look at cured pork products like salami and chorizo, for example:

The farmer plans for the boar and sow to mate, then the sow gives birth to piglets. The piglets are weaned, then the grown pig is sent to slaughter. The carcass is butchered, then the pork is sold to the customer. Now, with cured meat products, just before the pork is sold to the customer, an expert steps in and says, 'Hang on. Lend it to me for a bit and I'll use all my skills, resources and experience to make it into another product... then you can buy it'. It's like having a top chef step in and prepare your pork shoulder or your sirloin steak for you so that you can eat it immediately or just pop it in a recipe; they add taste and value to a product before it even reaches you.

The second reason is that I find it really tasty. Homo sapiens evolved to farm animals because we realized that, with limited food resources around us at the time, we could flee and/or fight for a lot longer if we'd eaten fats, protein, iron and vitamin B that day, as opposed to just leaves and berries. The strength we got from this diet became affiliated with our taste buds and food preferences, and we went searching for what is basically fuel. I realize it's a different world we live in today, and a sensible and educated approach to vegetarianism and even veganism is entirely possible, because we have an unlimited resource of food products, knowledge, supplements and food science to be able to compensate for the strength and energy that meat once gave us. However, it doesn't mean that the combination of salt, meat and fat doesn't still taste terrific to the taste buds I inherited from my cavewoman ancestors millions of years ago.

The third reason, funnily enough, comes from the very reason cured meat developed in the first place – out of necessity in man's battle against bacteria. Yes, I'm talking shelf-life, still the biggest commercial challenge in the food industry today. Curing and fermentation developed simultaneously around the globe in almost every culture and race (in many different forms) because we needed to find ways to preserve our food. We're spoilt for choice nowadays with technology in the home, but there's still a simple challenge when you buy some fresh meat on a Monday and your plans change during the week, so you still haven't eaten it by Friday. Given that it already took three days at the start of the logistics chain to get the meat from the abattoir to the supermarket or butcher's shop before it reached you... well, you're out of shelf-life. The really practical and wonderful joy of something like a stick of chorizo in your refrigerator, is that it lasts a long time. When you open your refrigerator and wonder what on earth you're going to have for supper that night (because you know you haven't been shopping for a bit!), you can whip up

a bowl of pasta with some sautéed shallots and diced chorizo, or make a quick tart with saucisson sec, or a nutritious fritatta with pancetta. Freezing is wonderful and helpful, but it's even easier to have some cured meat in the refrigerator that doesn't need defrosting. I think the really significant rise in its popularity in the last 10 years, outside of the Mediterranean countries where it has existed for centuries, is because we're all trying to waste less food; cured meat almost never gets thrown away.

Those are my three main reasons for loving charcuterie as I do, and it's the first reason that ensured this collection of recipes was such a pleasure to put together ... a pleasure and also a total dream because, well, what a fraud am I?! Months of care has been taken by somebody who cured the product, and I just swing in on the home stretch and form a recipe around it or pair it with accompaniments... and then I'm trying to take the credit. However, I'm not sorry, and I urge you to be the same, because I intend this collection to be a celebration of charcuterie and salumi and I have total admiration for the work done at the source of the meat curing. And like a good board of charcuterie, this book was going to be even better shared. I needed Louise's exquisite skills, creativity and passion to bring even more excitement and ideas to these pages. We both hope you enjoy this book as much as we enjoyed creating it.

Miranda & Louise

THE
BOARDS

Serving charcuterie boards

Due in part to recent exposure on social media, the trend to serve just one course, albeit in a variety of visually striking ways, is appealing for many reasons. Communal dining forms the very foundation of how we enjoy many different eating experiences, be it with friends for supper or work colleagues for dinner, a family party or even a wedding. Charcuterie boards are colourful, lavish, exciting and less time-consuming for the cook, and they are incredibly versatile, suiting all types of diets, culinary beliefs, times of day and occasions.

They are, however, not that new. Throughout central and southern Europe, the sharing of different types of food or dishes has long been enjoyed as an essential part of living, as well as an important part of our need to socialize. In France it is called apèro, in Spain it is tapas, Italy has antipasto, and meze is enjoyed all over the eastern Mediterranean, the Middle East and North Africa. All are ways of sharing a drink with small dishes of food ahead of a main meal, usually dinner (except meze, which is often the whole meal itself). Today's more creative and substantial boards take this concept and run with it, making dining less formal, more convivial and, I think, very 21st century.

Catering for guests can be quite stressful, but it doesn't need to be – and this is why charcuterie boards have really hit the spot for today's cook. They offer us a way to share our love of good food with flair and a sense of drama, without having to spend hours in the kitchen – and you don't need to be a great cook. There are no rules: anything goes. I think we all like to show off a little when it comes to entertaining, and with careful planning, you can create your own fabulous charcuterie boards fit for any occasion.

With our selection of themed boards to inspire you, why not unleash your inner creative genie and plan your next dinner party with an array of delicious charcuterie meats, cheese and accoutrements?

The practicalities

Here's a guide to help you through the different stages, from concept to table. Be it Christmas, a summer picnic, a birthday or wedding, your starting point will be numbers and quantities required.

- **What to serve your food on** – you will need boards or platters on which to arrange your chosen foods. This can be a well-loved kitchen chopping board, a new purchase, an old antique find or even a purpose-cut board from your local hardware store. It could be wooden, ceramic, slate, marble or perhaps metal. It can be round, square or rectangular; large or small. For 2–4 guests, use a small board; 6–8 people, a medium board; 12 or more, use a large board; and then for weddings or other large social gatherings, combine as many boards as you need.
- **Planning and shopping** – these are essential to sourcing quality ingredients. Choose the theme and then either use our suggestions as a template or just refer to it as a guide to inspire. Remember, shopping seasonally is important as is sourcing products locally when possible.
- **Slicing meats** – many hams and salamis are now available pre-sliced, although many delis or supermarkets stock whole meats that can be sliced to order. Of course you can buy your own meat slicer if you are a regular charcuterie eater – there is a wide range of different models available, ranging from really cheap manual options to top-end electric slicer models.
- **Design** – get inspired: use this book and other visual sources to fire the imagination. Some boards have an obvious theme such as Christmas, so perhaps a wreath or Christmas tree shape, whilst others are just more generic.

- **Balance** – you are looking to combine textures, colours and flavours as equally as you can. For a main-course platter, the following quantities provide a guide. If you are serving your board as a starter or as a pre-dinner appetizer, then reduce this by about a third.

Charcuterie: *50–75 g/2–3 oz. per person*
Cheeses: *25–50 g/1–2 oz. per person*
Fruit/veg: *a few slices per person*
Nuts: *a small handful per person*
Dried fruits: *2–4 pieces per person*
Sauces/dips: *2 tablespoons per person*
Bread/crackers: *100–150 g/3½–5 oz. per person*

- **Arranging the board** – gather all the ingredients in front of you. Pick the larger pieces, such as the cheeses, bread and bowls containing sauces, dips, spreads, pickles or olives, and place them well apart on the board. Fold or overlap slices of salami and ham, giving the ham a tweak upwards to add height to the board. Arrange each type of meat in groups with fans of salami in one spot and curls of ham in another. Try to avoid placing all the meats together. Add a few fresh herbs at this stage, placing them in the smaller gaps between the meats. Larger gaps are good for placing fruits, either whole or sliced, and the same goes for vegetables or salad leaves. Place crackers in baskets, on smaller boards or on the board itself. Finally, finish off by adding a flourish of fresh herbs or edible flowers. If you like, drizzle some honey over cheeses or soft salamis.

Remember, serving charcuterie boards is all about fun, enjoying the process and relaxing with friends and family. Entertaining just got a whole load easier.

ITALIAN CHARCUTERIE BOARD

It feels appropriate to kick off our charcuterie boards chapter with an Italian theme. After all, some of the best-known salume comes from Italy, who remain the largest producers of cured meats. I'll never forget the wafer-thin slices of prosciutto on my first ever antipasti platter – the combination of melt-in-the-mouth ham perfectly complemented by preserved artichokes and char-grilled (bell) peppers all in perfect harmony – that captured my heart.

Food products in Italy have a classification known as DOP or Denominazione di Origine Protetta (protected designation of origin), which is to guarantee that each product is produced and packaged according to its geographical location, as well as the traditions from that region. This includes charcuterie, as well as cheeses, wines and olive oils. With such a wide variety of products available, it is a good way to guarantee quality when sourcing your meats.

Italy produces wonderful salamis with each region having its own speciality. They range in size, as well as flavour, and can be long and thin, pressed into a brick shape or formed into a fat log. Aside from salamis, one of Italy's most famous and well-loved foods is prosciutto crudo or 'raw' ham. Served in thin slices either on its own, as part of an antipasti platter or with slices of melon, it is a true icon of Italian culinary history.

Charcuterie

As with all our charcuterie boards, the selection of cured meats has been assembled to provide the best combination for each theme. It is, however, only a guideline, and you can substitute these with different meats according to choice and availability.

- Prosciutto di Parma comes from Parma in northern Italy, is the crème de la crème of prosciutto crudo and has the DOP label to prove it. Produced from the whole hind leg of the pig, the meat is salted and left to hang for 1 year to cure – this is almost twice as long as other types of prosciutto crudo and it is this that gives the meat a drier texture and more buttery and nutty flavour. The flesh is a deep red with a vein of fat running through it. It should be served in wafer-thin slices.
- Coppa is a type of raw ham made from the muscle that runs from the nape of the pig down to the fourth or fifth rib. Here you will find the perfect balance of lean meat and fat. It is regarded as one of the finest Italian cured meats, originating in Calabria in southern Italy.
- Soppressata is a cured sausage made using leaner cuts of pork. The meat is more coarsely ground than some salami, with an even distribution of tiny fat particles. It is stuffed into a natural casing and is often flattened or pressed into a rectangular shape. It can be natural or spiced with chillies/chiles, giving it a rich colour.
- 'Nduja is a slightly different type of salami, far softer than most types of Italian salami, and is spread onto bread, rather than being sliced. Made from a highly spiced pork mixture, it comes from the southern region of Calabria at the foot of Italy. The vivid red colour is typical of the hot spicy Calabrian pepperoncini or hot chillies/chiles.
- Bresaola, unlike the majority of charcuterie, is air-dried beef fillet. It is first salted and seasoned with a mix of spices, then cured for several days before being washed and finally hung to dry for several months. The best beef is reared in the Valtellina region of Lombardy and, due to its higher protein content than pork, it is a leaner meat than many other charcuterie options.

Accompaniments

A well-constructed charcuterie board should include a combination of other ingredients that offer variety, as well as a good balance of flavour, texture and colour. So when deciding on what to serve alongside your salume, think about all these elements.

- Cheeses: mozzarella di bufala, aged Parmesan, ricotta
- Pickles/preserves: artichoke hearts, sun-dried tomatoes, roasted stuffed (bell) peppers, caperberries, olives
- Fruit/veg: green grapes, tomatoes
- Sauces: Homemade Pesto (see below)
- Bread/crackers: grissini, Garlic-y Bruschetta (see page 72)
- Herbs: basil

Homemade Pesto

50 g/2 oz. fresh basil leaves
1 garlic clove, crushed
2 tablespoons pine nuts
¼ teaspoon sea salt
6–8 tablespoons extra virgin
  olive oil
2 tablespoons freshly grated
  Parmesan cheese
freshly ground black pepper

MAKES 150 ML/⅔ CUP

Place the basil, garlic, pine nuts and sea salt in a pestle and mortar and grind to form a fairly smooth paste. Slowly add the oil until you reach the required texture, then finally add the cheese and pepper, to taste. Cover the surface and store in the refrigerator for up to 3 days.

SPANISH TAPAS BOARD

Tapas is one of Spain's greatest culinary traditions that can be traced back centuries to when local bar keepers would cover their customers' drinks with a slice of bread or ham in order to keep the flies off; the word 'tapa' means lid and comes from the verb tapear 'to cover'. Today tapas has evolved into more of a 'philosophy', a way of life, if you like, where we share food and wine with friends. Spreading far and wide beyond its borders, tapas is enjoyed around the world and lends itself perfectly to the creation of a tapas-style charcuterie board. It is most commonly served pre-dinner as an early evening appetizer or a light lunchtime meal.

Spanish charcuterie includes a wide range of different types of cured sausages, known collectively as embutidos, of which chorizo is probably the most well known. Varieties differ from thick or thin, plain or smoked, with some containing lean meat and some containing fatty meat. As with Italy, Spain has a fine tradition of producing wonderful cured hams, mainly from the more mountainous regions of southern Spain, as well as the Pyrenees.

Charcuterie

- **Chorizo** is a specific type of Spanish sausage that is cured with spices before it is fermented and then hung and air-dried. The resulting sausage can then be eaten 'raw' in thin slices like salami or sliced more thickly and pan-fried. Both are delicious. Made from coarsely minced pork, it is flavoured with garlic, paprika and salt and is classified as either picante (meaning spicy) or dulce (meaning sweet), depending on the heat and amount of paprika used.
- **Jamón Serrano** is to Spain what prosciutto di Parma is to Italy and is a delicious air-dried ham. It is produced from a breed of white pig reared using traditional methods that originated in the Sierra mountains – serrano is the Spanish word for sierra, which in turn means mountain range. Serrano ham has a more intense flavour than Italian prosciutto, with a deeper red-brown flesh.
- **Jamón Ibérico** is considered the king of hams, hardly surprising as it was originally reserved only for those of royal descent! Fortunately for us mere mortals, this is no longer the case. Produced from a smaller breed of black Ibèrico pig, it takes 2 years for them to mature enough to develop the necessary ratio of fat to meat. The pigs spend their final days gorging themselves on acorns, resulting in a ham with an incredibly complex flavour; at once nutty and sweet, with just the right amount of saltiness.
- **Fuet** is a traditional Catalan cured sausage made

with pork meat that is air-dried in a natural casing. It is a long thin sausage that can be eaten either with bread as tapas, or added to stews and soups. The flavour ranges from mild to very spicy, depending on the seasonings. It is sometimes coated with herbs and chillies/chiles.

Accompaniments

- Cheeses: Manchego, Cabrales, Idiazabal
- Tapas dishes: 'Sweet Patatas Bravas' (see page 69), Pan-fried Chorizo in Red Wine (see below), Marcona almonds
- Fruit/veg: cherry tomatoes, black grapes
- Pickles/preserves: piquillo peppers, caperberries
- Sauces: romesco sauce, quince paste (membrillo)
- Bread: char-grilled bread

Pan-fried Chorizo in Red Wine

125 g/4 oz. chorizo (dulce)
1–2 tablespoons red wine
25 g/1 oz. char-grilled roasted
   (bell) peppers, cut into thin strips
1 small garlic clove, finely chopped
a little chopped fresh parsley

SERVES 4

Cut the chorizo into 5-mm/¼-inch thick slices and place in a cold frying pan/skillet. Place over medium heat and, as soon as the fat is released, pour in the wine. Deglaze the pan for 30 seconds, then add the peppers, garlic and parsley. Top with a layer of foil or a lid and cook gently over very low heat for 15 minutes. Transfer to a bowl and serve with the rest of the charcuterie board.

FRENCH CHARCUTERIE BOARD

The French invented charcuterie, so it's hardly surprising that they have an entire shop dedicated to preserved pork meats. With such a choice, buying charcuterie in France can be overwhelming and quality varies from region to region. Look for those products marked with PGI or Protected Geographical Indication, as this will ensure it is a genuine product from a particular region made using traditional methods.

France produces many types of air-dried ham similar to Italian prosciutto, and these are categorized by quality. Jambon sec is produced from pigs reared using modern farming practices, and is considered an everyday ham, whereas jambon sec supérieur uses more traditional methods and is a finer product. At the top of the tree is jambon de Bayonne, which is produced in the Pays Basque region of South West France. Jambon blanc is a boiled ham where the boned leg is cured in brine and smoked before being boiled. It makes a great addition to a charcuterie board (though I've not included it here).

French salami is called saucisson sec and is made from the neck and shoulder muscles of pigs. The meat is minced/ground and combined with different aromatics from garlic, pepper and sea salt to cheese, spices, nuts and even truffles. Saucisson sec are hand-tied and left to hang and cure for 30 days. Aside from pork, you can also find duck, venison and wild boar varieties.

Pâtés, terrines and rillettes are also popular in France, and are made from pork, duck, chicken, rabbit, wild boar and venison.

Charcuterie

- Jambon de Bayonne is the most prized ham from the Pays Basque region of south west France. The pigs are raised on a natural diet of chestnuts, acorns and beechnuts, resulting in ham with a distinctive sweet, nutty flavour developed over a 12-month period of curing and drying.
- Saucisson sec with hazelnuts is just one of literally hundreds of French air-dried sausages or saucisson sec. Whole hazelnuts are added to the minced/ground pork mixture before being encased in a natural skin. When cut into thin slices little slivers of hazelnuts are spotted throughout the meat.
- Pork tenderloin is similar to Spanish lomo or Italian lonza, where the whole pork loin is cured and air-dried. It is a very lean charcuterie product and is best bought as a whole sausage to be thinly sliced just prior to eating.
- Wild game salami can be made from venison, duck and boar. This type of saucisson sec comes in a variety of sizes and all have a wonderfully intense flavour. The meat is a deep red; often the pieces of fat are diced a little larger to speckle the sausage.
- Chicken liver pâté is a good option for anyone who loves rich liver pâté, but is not comfortable eating foie gras (duck or goose liver). Buy ready-made chicken liver pâté or see the recipe on page 97.
- Pork rillettes is another great French classic made with slow-cooked meat pressed into a dish and chilled. It is coarser than a pâté. Great on baguettes with cornichons. Try the Pork Rillettes on page 105.

Accompaniments

Always provide a cross-section of cheeses and include cow's, goat's and sheep's milk cheeses; fresh cheese; hard or semi-hard cheeses; as well as a blue cheese.

- Cheeses: Comté, Camembert, Roquefort, goat's cheese
- Fruit/veg: grapes, pears, radishes
- Nuts: walnuts
- Pickles/preserves: cornichons, cocktail onions, hard-boiled quail's eggs
- Sauces: herb butter, Olive Tapenade (see page 62)
- Bread/crackers: baguette

NORTHERN EUROPEAN CHARCUTERIE BOARD

The further north one travels in Europe the more smoked charcuterie meats you encounter and this is largely due to damper weather conditions. Today producers use special drying rooms, but historically preserving meat relied on the drier and hotter climates of southern Europe and the Mediterranean, where meats were air-dried in barns or outdoors. The smoking process kills off bacteria that might otherwise thrive.

Germany and Poland, both larger producers of charcuterie, have enormous forested areas ideal for rearing pigs and wild boar, so it is little surprise that they have a proud tradition of producing some of the most delicious smoked pork sausage and cured and smoked hams.

The UK has a similar climate and has a tradition of curing and cooking hams as well as producing wonderful beef, venison and game salamis, pâtés and terrines. The UK has seen a recent charcuterie renaissance with an increase in smaller, passionate artisan food producers, using traditional methods of preserving all types of locally produced meats.

As an overview, northern European charcuterie boards should always include cooked hams, smoked sausages, terrines, pâtés and game pies.

Charcuterie

- Black Forest ham, as the name suggests, comes from The Black Forest in Germany. It has a distinctive smoky flavour and deep red colour, as it is boned, cured and then smoked over pine wood. It was given the EU Designated Origin protection, meaning that it can only be produced in that area.
- Mettwurst is a variety of sausage made throughout north east Europe. It can be prepared and eaten in a variety of ways: cooked, fried or 'raw' spread on rye bread with onions. Predominantly made with pork and veal, mettwurst sausage is combined with pepper, marjoram, allspice, thyme and mustard, and piped into a synthetic casing that is not to be eaten.
- Kielbasa is the generic name for a Polish sausage and is a staple of their cuisine. They come in dozens of varieties, some smoked and some fresh, and can be made with beef, turkey, lamb and chicken as well as pork. Every region has its own speciality.
- Wiltshire ham comes from a traditional method of preserving ham legs in Wiltshire in England. The original dry cure method was superseded in the 20th century and the boned leg is now cured in a brine for several days. It is then washed and boiled producing a wonderfully succulent, slightly fibrous cooked ham. It is available smoked or unsmoked. Both are delicious.
- Wild boar salami is produced throughout northern Europe due to the large swathes of forested areas. It has a rich flavour and a deep red colour speckled with small–medium sized pieces of fat. Very rich, it is best served in wafer-thin slices.
- Liver pâtés are popular throughout northern Europe and are commonly made with chicken livers. They are often flavoured with mushrooms or black truffles. Serve with crackers or baguette.

Accompaniments

- Cheeses: aged Cheddar, Stilton, Double Gloucester
- Fruit/veg: radishes, pears, blackberries
- Nuts: hazelnuts
- Pickles/preserves: cocktail onions, onion and chilli jam, fig chutney
- Sauces: wholegrain mustard, redcurrant jelly
- Bread/crackers: Home-baked Oatcakes (see page 70), rye bread

NEW YORK DELI BOARD

New York is fabulous for a whole range of wonderful reasons and one of these is the great American deli. I remember on my first trip to the city, it didn't take me long to head uptown (a less salubrious area than it is today) where some of the best delis were to be found. I just had to order myself my first pastrami on rye – and I was not disappointed.

Piled high with all types of cured meats, cheeses, sauces, pickles and sandwich breads, a typical NY deli is a corner shop, grocery store and sandwich shop rolled into one. With a rich cultural mix, delicatessens were able to provide local residents with foods from their homeland, including Italian salamis, Jewish bagels, Spanish jamón and a more American invention, luncheon meat. It means that charcuterie is a well loved part of New York cuisine and perfect for a themed charcuterie board.

Charcuterie

- Pastrami is a must on this charcuterie board. Originally from Romania, pastrami has been adopted by many countries around the world. A New York pastrami is made from beef navel or brisket. It is cured in brine and the meat is then coated with a spice mix, which includes garlic, coriander seeds, black pepper, paprika, cloves, allspice and mustard seeds. The meat is then smoked and served in thickish slices.
- Pepperoni sticks are mini sticks of salami, made using the end bits of pork, beef and bacon. They are the perfect meaty snack that were actually invented in the US. They come in all lengths and thicknesses, as well as different flavour combinations. Choose several different ones.
- Soppressata is an Italian salami that is beloved by Americans. It is a cured sausage made using leaner cuts of pork. It can be mild or spicy and most commonly in the US is formed into a round sausage shape rather than the flatter pressed version in Italy.
- Sliced pepper salami is a typical addition to many deli boards. The peppery crust is perfectly balanced by the soft, creamy centre.

Accompaniments

Make sure you balance your selection of meats with some sharp cheeses and sweet pickles.

- **Cheeses: Monterey Jack, Cheddar, Brie**
- **Fruit/veg: blueberries, lettuce**
- **Nuts: glazed pecans (see recipe below)**
- **Pickles/preserves: Caramelized Red Onions (see page 61), cornichons**
- **Sour Cream Slaw (optional: see page 57)**
- **Sauces: American mustard, Homemade Chipotle Ketchup (see page 65)**
- **Bread/crackers: breadsticks, crackers**

Glazed Pecans

150 g/1¼ cups pecan halves
4 tablespoons maple syrup
½ teaspoon sea salt
½ teaspoon smoked paprika
a pinch of cayenne pepper

Line a tray with baking parchment. Heat the pecans, maple syrup, salt, paprika and cayenne in a heavy-based frying pan/skillet on a medium heat until the liquid is boiling. Cook the nuts for 3–4 minutes until they are golden and glazed. Transfer immediately to baking parchment and let cool in a single layer. Once cool store in an airtight jar and use as required.

SMOKED CHARCUTERIE BOARD

Although all charcuterie is cured, not all of it is smoked. Curing meat renders it safe to eat, so once cured no cooking is necessary. There are two main types of smoked foods: those that are cold-smoked over low heat for hours and eaten 'raw' and those that are hot-smoked; a process where they are smoked over high heat for a shorter length of time, which cooks the meat. Both are delicious, but the majority of charcuterie is cold-smoked and eaten as it is.

You can choose to add other examples of smoked foods to your board, if you like. There are many to choose from and include cold-smoked cheeses, hot-smoked nuts and smoked garlic, to name just a few. Balance your board with plenty of pickles and sauces to cut through the richness provided by the smoking process, and add a selection of light and colourful fruits, vegetables and herbs.

Charcuterie

- Cold-smoked duck breast is first cured to make it safe before being cold-smoked to draw out excess water and add flavour. It is served very thinly sliced on a charcuterie board or it makes a perfect starter served on a bed of dressed salad leaves with a nut oil and fruit vinegar.

- Hot-smoked duck breast (see right) is smoked at a temperature that cooks the meat through. It takes about 15–20 minutes for an average size duck breast and it can be eaten hot, or left to go cold and sliced as part of a charcuterie platter.

- Hot-smoked chicken is available either as a whole bird, but more commonly as a whole smoked breast or pre-packaged in slices. It adds a lighter touch.

- Kabanos is a Polish cured sausage made with coarse minced/ground pork. Kabanos is made in long, slim links and lightly smoked. It can be eaten as it is, or it can be cooked.

- Chouriço is the Portuguese word for chorizo, but unlike its Spanish neighbour, this sausage has less paprika but more spice in the form of piri-piri. Another distinction is that Portuguese chouriço is almost always smoked after it is cured. It can be eaten 'raw' in slices but is often char-grilled over charcoal on the barbecue until the skin is quite charred. It is delicious.

- Smoked ham is a section of the leg of pork that is cured in a brine and then smoked over low heat for a long time to add flavour. It is then boiled and often roasted at a high temperature for 30 minutes before being sliced. In the UK it is traditional to serve it at Christmas.

Accompaniments

- Cheeses: Trappe smoked cheese, goat's cheese, Pyrenean mountain cheese
- Veg: radishes
- Nuts: pistachio nuts
- Pickles/preserves: Apple Slaw (see page 58), cornichons, cocktail onions
- Sauces: honey, Chunky BBQ Sauce (see page 64), redcurrant jelly
- Bread/crackers: selection of interesting crackers, dark rye bread

Hot-smoked Duck in a Wok

75 g/3 oz. long-grain rice
25 g/1 oz. black tea leaves
3 tablespoons soft brown sugar
1 large duck breast

SERVES 6

Take a heavy flameproof casserole and line it with a double layer of foil. Combine the rice, tea leaves and sugar together and spread it evenly over the base of the foil-lined pan. Place a rack or trivet over the top, about 3–4 cm/1¼–1½ inches above the rice. Cover with a tight-fitting lid and place the pan over high heat until you start to see wisps of smoke; 2–3 minutes.

Meanwhile, heat a dry frying pan/skillet over high heat. Add the duck, skin-side down and sear for 3 minutes, or until the skin is browned and much of the fat has melted.

Transfer the duck to the smoking pan, laying the breast skin-side down. Cover and reduce the heat to medium. Cook for 8 minutes. Turn off the heat but leave undisturbed for a further 10 minutes. Rest the duck for 5 minutes and serve hot. Or, if preferred, allow to cool completely and serve cold, in slices.

GAME CHARCUTERIE BOARD

Game is classified in two ways: feathered or furred. The first includes pheasant, grouse, partridge, pigeon and duck, whilst furred game includes venison, hare, rabbit and wild boar. Many cured game products are given classic charcuterie names such as salami, prosciutto and bresaola largely due to the processes being so similar. Today both wild and farmed game is made into charcuterie. Game is popular in countries that have a long history of meat preservation; wild animals were hunted, cured and dried so they could be eaten over the coming months when little fresh meat was available.

Wild boar numbers have been on the increase in Europe to such an extent that in some regions they have become a real danger to other wildlife and humans. Consequently this has led to more wild boar charcuterie production, mainly by quality artisan producers. Other typical types of salami are venison and duck, made with both wild and farmed animals. Rabbit and duck are often made into rillettes, whilst game terrines are commonplace in many countries, often mixing several types of game in a single terrine.

Charcuterie

- Duck prosciutto is a cured and air-dried duck breast. Although not strictly speaking prosciutto, it does share a resemblance. It is quick and easy to prepare but takes several weeks to air-dry the meat.
- Wild boar salami is a rich but not overly gamey meat. Romania and Transylvania in particular has a wonderful tradition of producing fabulous boar charcuterie. The region has the largest swathes of virgin forests in Europe, meaning wild boar roam free, perfect for local artisan charcuterie producers.
- Venison salami – venison is far leaner than pork and venison salami is full of wild game character with a rich meaty flavour. It is a deep ruby red colour and is mostly formed into long thin salamis.
- Duck salami is typically French as they have a huge love of all things 'canard'. Duck meat is rich with a lovely ruby red hue. It is typically made into quite thin, shortish saucisson sec.

- Game terrine is made with a base of minced/ground pork that is combined with 2–3 types of game meat, garlic, herbs, nutmeg and pepper. The raw meat mixture is pressed into a baking pan or ceramic dish and cooked in the oven. It is common to find rich game pâtés speckled with dried fruits and nuts, especially pistachios.

Accompaniments

Game goes really well with jellies, chutneys and jams, including the Fig Chutney on page 60.

- Cheeses: Camembert, aged Cheddar
- Fruit/veg: pears
- Nuts/dried fruits: walnuts, dried apricots
- Pickles/preserves: Fig Chutney (see page 60), Caramelized Red Onions (see page 61)
- Sauces: cranberry sauce
- Bread/crackers: Melba Toast (see page 73)

SUMMER PICNIC CHARCUTERIE BOARD

The sun is shining, the days are longer and the evenings balmy; it must be picnic time! Summer is a time to celebrate and it seems as if the stars are aligned; we are more sociable, we want to be outdoors and we are more spontaneous. We hanker for lighter dishes when it's hot: refreshing salads, cold meats, soft cheeses, crisp vegetables with a creamy mayonnaise. I can't think of many better ways to make the most of this than getting together with friends or family to share this sense of seasonal fun, and a summer charcuterie picnic is the perfect basis for this.

Although there will be little to no cooking involved in preparing your charcuterie board, you will need to take a moment to plan how you will transport everything to the picnic. Charcuterie meats, once sliced, should be kept chilled along with any other foods that will spoil in the heat, so prepare them in advance and store under food wraps in the fridge until the last minute. If your fridge is large enough you can arrange much of your ingredients on your board (or platter), cover tightly and keep chilled, ready to go. Alternatively arrange the foods in groups and store in separate containers to arrange on your board at your picnic table.

Charcuterie

- **Prosciutto di Parma (Parma ham)** tends to have a lighter flavour than some of the other types of air-dried hams from Spain and France. Choose wafer-thin slices if you are buying ready-sliced or ask your butcher to slice them as thinly as possible.
- **Lomo or lonza** is a perfect summer charcuterie meat. The pork loin fillet is cured as a whole piece rather than minced/ground and the resulting meat is leaner than salamis. Ideal for summer, it is traditionally served in thin slices and served with some bread.
- **Mortadella (known as Bologna in the US)** is a large Italian sausage that is more like a cold cut of meat, than salami; it is made from cooked cured pork. It is often flavoured with pistachio nuts, which add a lovely spike of green in the pretty pink meat. It is sliced wafer-thin.

- **Smoked chicken breast** should retain its moisture and result in a smoky but still succulent meat. It is delicious accompanied by a creamy mayonnaise and salad leaves.
- **Rabbit terrine** is a less intensely flavoured terrine, more like a pâté de campagne than a game terrine. It is often baked in small dishes, then chilled and served straight from the dish. It is a lighter terrine ideal for summer.
- **Baby salamis** – you can find several different types of mini salami sticks as well as rather cute little barrels or mini sausages. They are a fun addition to any charcuterie board.

Accompaniments

Meats don't need to take a back seat but make sure you pair them with plenty of lighter touches, with fresh summer fruits, berries and tender salad leaves.

- Cheeses: herbed and fruit goat's cheese
- Fruit/veg: mango slices, baby vegetables, cherry tomatoes, strawberries, redcurrants, cos leaves
- Nuts: pistachios,
- Sauces: Saffron Mayonnaise (see page 93)
- Breads: breadsticks
- Herbs: micro herbs, edible flowers

FESTIVE CHARCUTERIE BOARD

The festive season brings people together and provides the perfect opportunity to show off your creative skills and to wow your guests with a show-stopper charcuterie board on your Christmas table. There are lots of different inspirational references to draw upon to transform your board into a winter wonderland of shapes, colours and, of course, seasonal flavours. Include the finest hams, salamis and cheeses that are at their best during the cooler months. Grocery stores are full of colourful tangerines, cranberries, figs and other fresh gems, whilst Christmas preserves, chutneys, nuts and crackers abound.

It is also one time that we feel happy to splurge a bit, treating ourselves to ingredients we may not normally consider. The arrival of certain foods often coincides with this time of year, foods which have now become part of a Christmas tradition. Others just happen to be seasonal and therefore at their peak during the winter months.

In a homage to Christmas traditions, why not arrange everything as a Christmas wreath or an even more kitsch Christmas tree. Use a round board to guide your wreath shape, adding splashes of colour with herbs and berries. A rectangular board is best for a tree shape, arranging things in rows with dried fruits and nuts to separate the meats. Enjoy.

Charcuterie

- Jamón Ibérico, prosciutto di Parma and jambon de Bayonne: all of these three products represent the best quality prosciutto of their respective countries, and they all contain unique characteristics. Treat yourself to all three for your Christmas board.
- Bresaola is air-dried beef fillet from Italy, but if you have the chance to treat yourself to Wagyu bresaola, do! Wagyu is a breed of beef cattle originally from Japan and the meat contains a higher percentage of omega-3 and omega-6 fatty acids and monounsaturated fats than other breeds. Due to the more evenly spread veins of fat that run through wagyu beef, the meat is exceptionally tender. The resulting bresaola is a wonderfully delicate, soft and delicious meat.
- Black truffle salami are produced in France and Italy in the regions where truffles are commonly found. Pieces of black truffle are combined with the sausage mix to air-dry and cure. The resulting salami is a deeper ruby colour with a wonderfully slightly earthy sweet/savoury flavour. Unforgettable.
- Game pie is similar to a terrine, but cooked in a pastry crust. A mixture of pork, game meat, spices, liver and pepper are combined and pressed into a loaf pan lined with a hot water crust pastry, and is then cooked. It is filled with a rich aspic, left to go cold and served in slices with cranberry sauce.
- Dried Cranberry and Brandy Christmas Pâté (see page 101) is a richly flavoured, lightly spiced pork and liver pâté spiked with dried cranberries. A splash of brandy adds an extra hit of Christmas flavour. Perfect with Melba Toast (see page 73).

Accompaniments

Mont d'Or is a rich cow's milk cheese from France only available during the cooler months of the year; it is traditionally baked in the oven until the creamy centre melts to a liquid gold. It is the perfect cheese to serve for a Christmas treat and an ideal melting pot for all the charcuterie ingredients.

- **Cheeses:** Mont d'Or (see recipe below), aged Parmesan, Tête de Moine (a cheese traditionally cut on a Girolle machine or cheese curler)
- **Fruit:** clementines, fresh cranberries
- **Nuts:** glazed pecans (see page 28)

- **Sauces:** Cranberry and Port Sauce (see page 64)
- **Bread/crackers:** selection of crackers, truffle crisps
- **Herbs:** bay leaves, rosemary, sage

Baked Mont D'Or

1 Mont d'Or cheese, at room temperature
2 garlic cloves, thinly sliced
2 rosemary sprigs
60 ml/¼ cup Jura wine
1 tablespoon extra virgin olive oil
freshly ground black pepper

baking dish, lined with baking parchment

SERVES 4

Preheat the oven to 190°C (375°F) Gas 5.

Remove the wooden lid of the cheese box. Make lots of small cuts into the top of the cheese and carefully poke in the garlic slices and rosemary sprigs. Pour the wine and olive oil over the cheese and season with pepper.

Place in the lined baking dish and bake in the preheated oven for 15–20 minutes, or until the cheese is really heated through and molten.

Transfer to your charcuterie board and serve with the bread, ham, figs, etc., to dip into the cheese.

CAL-ITAL CHARCUTERIE BOARD

Cal-Ital, short for Californian-Italian, first came to prominence in the 1850s when wine growers in California began planting Italian grape varieties. Both the climate and the soil conditions were similar to those in Italy, making it an ideal place for cultivating Italian grapes. California also had a significant Italian immigrant population who had arrived at the beginning of the gold rush. Together, these two factors influenced the love that Californians have for Italian wines and food.

So, what makes this board different to a traditional Italian charcuterie board? In truth there is little when it comes to the meats themselves. Nowadays the origin of the charcuterie is just as likely to be produced locally, often by small artisanal producers rather than imported from Italy. They may even share the same names. The main difference in the characteristics of a typical Californian charcuterie board is what else you serve alongside the meats.

In Italian cuisine, tradition is paramount. Not so for Californians who have a rich multicultural society from which to draw inspiration. Cheeses may come from local suppliers or be imported, whilst fruits and vegetables are generally available throughout the year. California is a place that not only accepts but encourages change and diversity. This board reflects the happy-go-lucky lifestyle of Californians in the sunshine state.

- 'Nduja is a spicy but spreadable salami originally from Calabria in southern Italy. It is delicious spread onto slices of lightly char-grilled ciabatta. Traditionally 'nduja is served drizzled with honey and here it is paired with truffle honey for a little extra bling.
- Coppa is a type of raw ham made from the muscle that runs from the nape of the pig down to the fourth or fifth rib. Here you will find the perfect balance of lean and fat meat. It is regarded as one of the finest Italian cured meats originating in Calabria in southern Italy
- Finocchiona is a robust salami flavoured with fennel and has a deeper colour than many Italian-style salamis. Originally from Tuscany, it is a popular addition to Californian charcuterie.
- Baby salami – you can find several different types of mini salami sticks as well as rather cute little barrels or mini sausages. They are a fun addition to any charcuterie board.

Charcuterie

- Guanciale, whose name is derived from the Italian for cheek, is a pork jowl or cheek similar to pancetta (although that is made from pork belly). Guanciale has a higher fat quantity, which gives the meat a rich, buttery flavour and wonderful balance between sweet and savoury. Sliced wafer-thin, it simply melts in the mouth.
- Salumi Chips (see page 77) may not be traditional, but they are fun, adding a lovely bite of texture in contrast to the other meats. They are literally thin slices of your favourite salumi baked until crisp.

Accompaniments

- Fruit/veg: grapes, cherry tomato and basil salad, rocket/arugula, physalis
- Dried fruits: mission figs
- Pickles/preserves: Warm Infused Olives (see page 66)
- Sauces: truffle honey
- Bread/crackers: Garlic-y Bruschetta (see page 72), vegetable crisps

ISLAND HOPPING CHARCUTERIE BOARD

There are a host of islands that lie in the Mediterranean and although some are Italian, some Spanish and some French, each of them is fiercely independent and extremely proud of their own unique culinary heritage. They share a similar climate, terrain and agricultural growing conditions to their mainland counterparts, so their charcuterie shares similar characteristics whilst maintaining their own methods of production.

Concentrating on the larger of the islands, this board shines a light on some of the finest cured meat products paired with other locally produced ingredients, including cheeses, aromatics and wines. The wild and often harsh terrain of these islands are home to numerous species of animals that are reared in the time-honoured pastoral tradition. These include sheep, goats, wild boar and, of course, pigs. These islands are a rich treasure trove of wonderful and sometimes totally unique foods.

Corsica, once part of Italy, is now French and is world-renowned for the quality of its charcuterie due to the native black pig (porcu nustrale). Exceptionally hardy, they have adapted well to modern breeding methods and roam free in forested areas gorging on a diet of chestnuts, acorns, insects and fruit.

The Spanish Balearic isles, which include Majorca and Menora, produce fine cheese and sausages, including a wonderful soft salami called sobrasada that can be spread onto bread, much like the Italian 'nduja.

Sicily produces some fine salami and one in particular, renowned for its flavour, is lardo (Italian for lards), which is produced using the meat from a breed of free-range black pigs typical of the hilly region of Nebrodi in the province of Messina. Sardinia also has a wonderful salami-making tradition and is particularly renowned for their cured sausages salsiccia Sarda. These are considered the ultimate Sardinian cured meat product.

Charcuterie

- Lardo is cured fat mainly produced from the back of the pig. The fat is cured in salt and herbs and allowed to air-dry for at least a month. It is either just a strip of fat or lard, or it can have a fine line or two of pale pink meat running through it, much like pancetta. It should be sliced very thinly.
- Sobrasada is a soft chorizo unique to the Balearic islands and Majorca in particular. It s similar to the Italian spreadable salami 'nduja and is also spicy.
- Salsiccia Sarda Tradizionale is a traditional Sardinian sausage. It is lightly spiced with black pepper, but has a distinct rich flavour. It works well with pecorino sardo on a charcuterie platter.
- Figatellu is a specialty from Corsica and is a raw blood sausage that must be cooked before it is eaten. It is U-shaped, about 30 cm/12 inches in length and is traditionally char-grilled on a barbecue before being slapped between chunky bread rolls.

Accompaniments

Many of these same islands produced some fabulous cheese, so make these a highlighted part of your board.

- Cheeses: pecorino sardo, Corsican Brin d'Amour
- Fruit/veg: cherry tomatoes, rocket/arugula, lemons
- Nuts: Marcona almonds
- Pickles/preserves: Puttanesca Relish (see page 62), lupins (a type of Italian bean served as part of an antipasti platter)
- Sauces: honey
- Bread/Crackers: Carta di Musica (Sardinian crispbreads), Crostino (see page 72)
- Herbs: thyme

KOSHER CHARCUTERIE BOARDS

The consumption of pork is forbidden under Jewish laws and therefore charcuterie must be derived from animals other than pigs, which are not considered kosher. Kosher charcuterie can be made using other types of meat, including beef, lamb, venison and goat, as well as poultry. Despite dairy products being kosher, they cannot be eaten with meat, therefore cheese and charcuterie cannot be put together on a board.

In countries that have a long history of producing charcuterie (such as France, Spain and Italy), we know Jewish communities have been preserving duck and goose as prosciutto as far back as the 15th century. Today kosher charcuterie includes a host of non-pork salamis, sausages, rillettes, pâtés, prosciutto and cold cuts. Certain products such as pastrami are traditionally made using beef, but always check packaging of all charcuterie products to make sure the product is kosher. Fortunately access to kosher ingredients is now far easier with many online suppliers, but if you can, shop locally.

Charcuterie

- Beef prosciutto is similar to beef pastrami but it is air-dried rather than brined and slow-cooked. It is available from online stores and makes for a fine alternative for a kosher charcuterie board. You could also use classic beef pastrami.
- Beef jerky can be traced back to the Quechua Indians, a Peruvian tribe during Inca times. They called it ch'arki or 'to burn meat'. The process involved drying the strips of meat on hot sunny days and alternately freezing it during cold sub-zero nights. It was adopted by American cowboys who used it to sustain themselves on long cattle drives. Today it is considered an American product.
- Bresaola is usually a beef or veal product, although you can also find venison and lamb bresaola. All of these work well on a kosher charcuterie board, offering lean meat with a rich flavour.

- Beef salami is somewhat less common, but again it is available as an alternative to the more usual pork varieties. It has a similar flavour to traditional salami but is less red in colour with a more mild taste. It is available from larger supermarkets, kosher food producers online, delis or local artisan producers. Duck and venison salamis could be substituted.
- Veal pancetta is a perfect substitute for the more traditional pork pancetta and, although it is often cooked in the same way as bacon is, it can be served 'raw' in thin slices, as it has been cured and air-dried.
- Chicken liver mousse – to be considered a kosher product, chicken livers must be totally cooked through before they are then made into a pâté or mousse. So it is essential to check the packaging if you are buying it, or make our version on page 97.

Accompaniments

- Fruit/veg: strawberries, avocados, apples, green grapes
- Pickles/preserves: Pickled Cucumbers (see opposite), Sauerkraut (see page 56), beetroot pickles, cornichons, olives
- Sauces: wholegrain mustard
- Bread/crackers: dark rye bread, salted pretzels, bagel crisps

Pickled Cucumbers

1 pickling cucumber
   (e.g., ridge cucumber
   or gherkin)
3 tablespoons sea salt
1 garlic clove, chopped
1 shallot, chopped
2 bay leaves
a pinch of dried cinnamon
3 tablespoons distilled
   white vinegar
freshly ground black pepper

MAKES 1 JAR (200 G/7 OZ)

Slice the cucumber either crossways or lengthways and lay it on a plate. Sprinkle 1 tablespoon of salt over the top and leave for 1 hour, to draw out a lot of the moisture.

Rinse the cucumber slices and pat dry with paper towels. Sterilize a jar, and then put the cucumber slices into the jar.

Put 200 ml/generous ¾ cup water and the remaining salt into a saucepan and bring to the boil to make a brine. Remove from the heat and let cool a little, so it's not boiling hot.

Add the garlic, shallot, bay leaves, cinnamon and a pinch of black pepper to the jar, and shake. Add the vinegar, then pour the brine over the top.

Seal the lid and leave in the refrigerator for 2–3 days before serving.

MEZE CHARCUTERIE BOARD

Popular throughout eastern Mediterranean countries, North Africa and the Middle East, meze is a collection of small appetizers served on the table in individual dishes, in much the same way as Spanish tapas, Italian antipasti and French apéro. The word itself comes from the Arabic term t'mazza which translates as 'to savour in little bites'. Aside from the wonderful flavours, textures and colours provided by meze, the sharing of food with friends and family is a celebration of community and appreciation of fabulous ingredients lovingly prepared and commonplace in all these countries.

Perhaps the most colourful of all boards, we can combine some really wonderful fresh ingredients alongside some carefully chosen charcuterie. Because of religious beliefs, pork is not eaten in some of the countries that traditionally serve meze, however others, such as Greece, Romania, Bulgaria and Albania all have a rich history of curing meats including pork. You can choose whichever suits you.

Charcuterie

- Merguez sausages, made with minced/ground lamb or beef are not strictly charcuterie as they are fresh, although occasionally they are sun-dried. Packed full of wonderful spices including harissa, which gives them their red colour, as well as sumac, fennel and garlic, they are a deliciously smoky sausage with a wonderful flavour when char-grilled.
- Sucuk or sujuk is a type of dry, spiced sausage similar to salami and is salty, dry and has a high fat content. It is traditionally made using minced/ground beef and is combined with spices such as garlic, salt, cumin, sumac and red pepper before being piped into a casing. It can be served raw but is more commonly pan-fried.
- Pastrama is where American pastrami first originated, but there are differences. Romanian pastrama is a cured, semi-dried smoked meat that can be made from beef, pork, lamb or, in fact, pretty much any type of meat. It resembles prosciutto more than American pastrami. If you can, try lamb pastrama which is less common, but truly delicious.

- Lefkada salami is a mixed pork and beef salami from the Greek Island of Lefkada, where it has been traditionally made for centuries. It is thought to have been introduced by Venetians and is similar to many Italian salamis, any of which could be used instead.

Accompaniments

What sets a meze board apart from other boards in this book is the amount of wonderful side dishes you can serve alongside the meat to complement and enhance it. You can often buy ready-made products, including hummus, tahini and tabbouleh, or make your own.

- Cheeses: feta, halloumi
- Fruit: pomegranates
- Nuts/dried fruits: pistachios, dried apricots, dates
- Pickles/preserves: pickled chillies/chiles, olives, preserved lemons
- Sauces/dips: hummus, tahini
- Bread/crackers: flatbreads
- Herbs/salad: tabbouleh

BUTTER BOARDS

Are butter boards the new charcuterie boards? If you are a fan of food trends and TikTok, then you'll likely know what they are. For the uninitiated, of which I was one, let's take a closer look. Firstly spread a clean and sterilized chopping board with softened butter to cover it completely and then scatter over your chosen toppings. These can vary from fresh herbs, olives, nuts and dried fruits to just about anything you want, including, of course, charcuterie. All you need then is a hunk of bread, so you dunk in and eat — it's kind of fast food on steroids.

Despite the sudden social media attention, the practice isn't that revolutionary. The French have been serving radishes and sea salt with pats of butter for years; whilst in Middle Eastern cuisine, spreads such as hummus and tahini are regularly served drizzled with oil and topped with spices, herbs and even meat, so the diner can simply dip some flatbread in and scoop up a perfect mouthful of wonderful flavours. There are even restaurants who have been serving butter boards for a while now, so the trend is likely to grow.

This idea may not be to everyone's liking, but it can work well, especially with a carefully selected combination of ingredients. To avoid double dipping, I prefer to arm my guests with a knife, so they can spread the topping rather than scooping it directly from the board.

Charcuterie

In order to make the scooping or spreading up of the butter and topping in one, it is best to choose smaller pieces of meat, so choose appropriately.

- Chorizo can either be sweet or hot for this. Go for a thinner one, as it is easier to scoop onto your bread.
- Fuet salami is a Spanish salami that is long and thin, making it an ideal choice here. We have used three different flavours for the board opposite.
- Prosciutto in wafer-thin slices is perfect for a butter board, or alternatively you can use jamón Serrano or jambon sec instead (but cut it into strips to make it easier to scoop and eat).

Accompaniments

Because you have a layer of butter already on your board (you can use salted or unsalted, but remember charcuterie is already high in salt, so perhaps unsalted is a safer option) avoid any soft cheeses, soft pâtés or spreadable salamis.

- **Cheeses:** Double Gloucester, Stilton
- **Fruit/veg:** radishes, cherry tomatoes, celery
- **Nuts/dried fruits:** raisins, pistachio nuts
- **Pickles/preserves:** olives
- **Sauces:** honey, maple syrup, reduced balsamic vinegar
- **Bread/crackers:** selection of crackers, baguette

Alternative board ideas

- Spread a platter with some soft goat's curd and top with slices of smoked duck prosciutto, chopped fresh herbs, rocket/arugula and a drizzle of fruity olive oil and reduced balsamic vinegar
- Spread a platter with hummus and top with sautéed chorizo, olives, char-grilled (bell) peppers and sun-dried tomatoes, parsley, coriander/cilantro, preserved lemon, honey and black sesame seeds
- Cut open three whole burratas onto a large plate and top with strips of prosciutto, baby broad/fava beans, shredded radicchio, fresh basil leaves and a drizzle of fruity extra virgin olive oil

ACCOMPANIMENTS
FOR BOARDS

Sauerkraut

Sauerkraut is a fine (and very easy) example of fermenting, and it's delicious with hot meat, like sausages, or spooned onto a mouthful of cured meat.

1 green cabbage (I recommend Savoy Cabbage)
2 tablespoons sea salt
1 tablespoon caraway seeds

**MAKES 1 JAR
(ABOUT 200 G/7 OZ.)**

Remove an outer leaf of the cabbage, rinse and set aside – don't worry if it tears a bit.

Chop the cabbage into thin slices, removing the stalk in the middle.

In a mixing bowl, sprinkle the salt and caraway seeds over the cabbage, and then massage with your hands for 5 minutes, squeezing the salt into the cabbage so that it reduces and starts to draw out the moisture. Set aside for at least 1 hour, until more water is drawn out and gathers at the bottom.

Sterilize a jar, and then put the cabbage and liquid in the jar. If you have more than about 4–5 tablespoons of liquid, drain a little bit away. (The liquid shouldn't come higher than the cabbage.)

Squash the cabbage down in the jar and then push the reserved leaf down on top, so that there is air above the leaf but no gap below it.

Store at room temperature for 3–4 days, then transfer to the refrigerator for 1 day before serving. Store in the refrigerator for up to 1 month.

Sour Cream Slaw

A tangy and fresh alternative to a traditional coleslaw and a great (optional) addition to the New York Deli board on page 28.

125 g/2 cups shredded white cabbage

125 g/2 cups shredded red cabbage

175 g/generous 1¼ cups grated carrots

½ white onion, thinly sliced

1 teaspoon salt

2 teaspoons caster/superfine sugar

1 tablespoon white wine vinegar

50 g/scant ¼ cup mayonnaise

50 g/scant ¼ cup sour cream

MAKES 500 G/6 CUPS

Place the white and red cabbage, carrots and onion in a colander and sprinkle with the salt, sugar and vinegar. Stir well and then leave to drain over a bowl for 20 minutes.

Mix together the mayonnaise and sour cream, then combine with the cabbage, carrots and onion. Serve immediately or cover and keep refrigerated for up to 2 days.

Sweet & Feisty Crème Fraîche

This is lovely served with the Slow-cooked, Dry-rub Pork Ribs with BBQ Sauce (see page 160), for example. It's got a bit of a kick but also a sweetness and freshness, so it's ideal to soften a rich serving of cured meat.

2 tablespoons crème fraîche/ sour cream

1 teaspoon chipotle powder

4 pinches of cayenne pepper

2 teaspoons maple syrup

SERVES 4

Put all the ingredients into a bowl and stir to mix them together. Serve immediately or cover and keep refrigerated for up to 2 days.

Celeriac Remoulade

½ celeriac/celery root, peeled
    and grated
freshly squeezed juice of ½ lemon
    (see Cook's Note)
1 teaspoon mustard (Dijon/French
    or wholegrain are best)
a big pinch of freshly chopped
    parsley
a pinch of fennel seeds
a pinch of sea salt

SERVES 4

Combine all the ingredients in a bowl, mixing them together well, and chill in the refrigerator, covered, for at least 1 hour before serving so that the flavours can be absorbed.

Cook's Note
Add the freshly squeezed juice of ½ lemon first and then taste and add a little more, if you like.

Apple Slaw

You'll see quite a lot of sour or acidic ingredients in the accompaniments and the recipes. They go so well with the rich, salty salumi, so it really reaches the far sides of your taste buds. Here's a slaw recipe with a sour apple taste.

1 tablespoon cider vinegar
2 tablespoons mayonnaise
¼ white cabbage, cored and
    shredded
1 carrot, grated
4–5 spring onions/scallions,
    finely chopped
a big pinch of freshly chopped
    parsley
2 eating/dessert apples, cored
    and coarsely grated (leave
    the peel on)
sea salt and freshly ground
    black pepper

SERVES 2-3

Pop all the ingredients into a bowl and mix well. Be sure to taste the slaw and then adjust the seasoning and add more of anything to suit your taste. Cover and refrigerate until you are ready to serve.

Try to make this at least 1 hour before serving, so that you can chill it really well and allow the flavours to mingle – this creates a delightful contrast with salumi.

Fig Chutney

Enjoy this sticky, sweet and mildly spiced fig chutney alongside pâté and homemade crackers or your favourite cheese. Make the most of fresh figs when they're in season!

25 g/2 tablespoons butter
1 red onion, finely diced
12 fresh figs, peeled and chopped
40 g/1½ oz. soft/packed brown sugar
3 tablespoons red wine vinegar
a pinch of ground ginger
a handful of sultanas/golden raisins
freshly squeezed juice of ¼ lemon

**MAKES 1 JAR
(ABOUT 200G/7 OZ.)**

Melt the butter in a frying pan/skillet, then add the onion and fry over fairly high heat until it's soft and starting to brown. Stir in the figs and sugar, then add the vinegar, ginger and sultanas/golden raisins. Add the lemon juice and 3 tablespoons water. Reduce the heat to a low simmer and cook, uncovered, for 10–15 minutes, until the mixture thickens, stirring occasionally.

Remove from the heat and let cool, then transfer to a sterilized jar or a suitable airtight container and cover. Store in the refrigerator. It is best to make this chutney at least 24 hours before serving, to allow the flavours to mature.

Cook's Note
This chutney will keep (if sealed) for a couple of weeks in the refrigerator. You can also freeze it (in an airtight container). Just check the flavour after you defrost it, as it might need a little top-up of seasoning – perhaps a little more ground ginger or a squeeze of fresh lemon juice.

1 red onion, thinly sliced
2 tablespoons runny honey

SERVES 2

Preheat the oven to 180°C
(350°F) Gas 4.

Put the onion in an
ovenproof dish (see Cook's
Note), drizzle over the honey
and stir to mix so that the
onions are well coated.

Roast in the preheated
oven for about 15 minutes until
caramelized. Roast for longer
if you want them chewy and
crispy. If you're doing a bigger
batch, it's worth giving them
a shimmy around so that they
all get a chance to caramelize.

You can freeze this in
portions for 6 months, or it'll
keep in the refrigerator in a
sealed container for up to
2 weeks.

Cook's Note
These caramelized onions get
very sticky, so I tend to line the
ovenproof dish with foil, with
the edges folded in, so that I
can throw it away, rather than
scrub sticky onions off the dish.

Caramelized Red Onions

Easy peasy caramelizey. Something that can be an
accompaniment or as part of a recipe (see Tarte au
Saucisson Sec on page 144), and they last a couple of
days in a sealed container in the refrigerator, too.

Puttanesca Relish

This relish is quite like the Olive Tapenade (see below), but it's lighter and not as rich. It can be used to add to sandwiches and recipes, but it's also lovely served with a charcuterie board and spooned onto the meats.

50 g/2 oz. pitted black
    or Kalamata olives
2 canned anchovy fillets, drained
2 teaspoons capers, drained
a big pinch of freshly chopped
    coriander/cilantro
½ garlic clove
1 tablespoon olive oil
200-g/7-oz. can of tomatoes,
    drained (so you just have the
    pulp without too much liquid)
sea salt and freshly ground
    black pepper

MAKES 1 JAR
(ABOUT 200 G/7 OZ.)

Pop all the ingredients into a food processor and whizz until the pieces are nice and small and the texture is relatively smooth. I still like a few small chunks, so I stop before it becomes more like a purée.

Transfer the mixture to a small, sterilized jar or an airtight container, or divide it between two ramekins and cover.

This relish will keep for a week or two in a sealed container in the refrigerator. It is also suitable for freezing. If you do freeze it, defrost it slowly in the refrigerator and then taste before you serve it, topping up any of the flavours that you think need a boost – perhaps the coriander/cilantro or the garlic.

Cook's Note
If you're eating this relish straight away, you can mix in a little crème fraîche/sour cream to make it slightly creamy, if you like. This won't then keep beyond a day in the refrigerator though, so only mix it in just before you serve it.

Olive Tapenade

This is a great mixture to have in a jar in the refrigerator to add to boards.

50 g/2 oz. pitted black olives
2 canned anchovy fillets, drained
1 teaspoon capers, drained
1 tablespoon olive oil
a squeeze of fresh lemon juice
5 fresh basil leaves
1 teaspoon tomato purée/paste
sea salt and freshly ground
    black pepper

MAKES 1 JAR
(ABOUT 200 G/7 OZ.)

Pop all the ingredients into a food processor and whizz until the pieces are nice and small and the texture is relatively smooth. I still like a few small chunks, so I stop before it becomes more like a purée.

Transfer the mixture to a small, sterilized jar or an airtight container, or divide it between two ramekins and cover.

This tapenade keeps for at least a week in a sealed container in the refrigerator. It is also suitable for freezing in portions. If you do freeze it, defrost it slowly in the refrigerator and taste before you serve it – you might like to add a little more basil or a squeeze more lemon juice.

Chunky BBQ Sauce

I don't know about you, but a poor-quality BBQ sauce can ruin a great plate of meat for me. It's so easy to make it at home and I hope you taste the difference (and delight in it) when enjoying fresh BBQ sauce as quickly as I did.

50 g/3½ tablespoons butter
1 onion, chopped
2 teaspoons tomato purée/paste
2 tablespoons soft/packed brown
    sugar
1 teaspoon paprika
a pinch of chipotle powder
2 teaspoons Worcestershire sauce
1 teaspoon English/hot mustard
    powder
2 tablespoons white wine vinegar
sea salt and freshly ground
    black pepper

**MAKES ABOUT
125 ML/½ CUP**

Melt the butter in a frying pan/skillet over medium heat, then add the onion and fry until soft and browned. Add the tomato purée/paste, sugar, paprika and chipotle powder, and stir well. Add the Worcestershire sauce, mustard powder and vinegar, and season with salt and pepper, then as soon as it bubbles, pour in 150 ml/⅔ cup water. Increase the heat to high and bring to the boil, then let it boil hard, uncovered, for about 10 minutes, until the mixture reduces and thickens.

Remove from the heat and let cool, then whizz it in a food processor. I like to keep BBQ sauce nice and chunky, but you can keep whizzing until it's smooth, if you prefer.

Cranberry & Port Sauce

An indulgent addition to the Festive Charcuterie Board on page 38.

1 cinnamon stick, bruised
1 star anise
3 whole cloves
500 g/4 cups frozen cranberries
250 g/1¼ cups granulated sugar
grated zest and juice of 1 orange
125 ml/½ cup Ruby Port
½ vanilla pod

**MAKES 2 X 350 G/
12-OZ. JARS**

Wrap the cinnamon stick, star anise and cloves in a small piece of muslin and tie it up with kitchen string. Place the cranberries, sugar, orange zest and juice, Port, vanilla pod and spice bag in a saucepan and heat gently, stirring until the sugar dissolves. Bring to the boil and simmer gently for 20 minutes until the cranberries are softened.

Using a slotted spoon remove about a half of the cranberries and set aside. Continue to cook the rest for a further 10 minutes until the mixture is syrupy. Discard spice bag and vanilla pod. Stir in the reserved cranberries and then spoon the mixture into 2 sterilised jars. Seal and allow to cool.

Homemade Chipotle Ketchup

This is lovely and light, and is perfect to serve with heavier main course/entrée dishes . This recipe makes plenty for a large gathering.

20 g/generous 1 tablespoon butter

1 onion, chopped

1 cooking apple, peeled, cored and chopped

1 teaspoon chipotle powder

2 teaspoons paprika

1 teaspoon sea salt

100 ml/⅓ cup cider vinegar

3 x 400-g/14-oz. cans of chopped tomatoes

100 g/scant ½ cup soft/packed brown sugar

MAKES ABOUT 500 G/1¼ LBS.

Melt the butter in a saucepan over medium heat and fry the onion until soft. Add the apple and continue to cook, stirring, for another minute or two. Add the chipotle powder, paprika and salt, then stir in the vinegar and bring to the boil.

Drain off about half of the juice from the cans of tomatoes – you don't need that much juice – then add the rest of the canned tomatoes and juice to the pan. Bring to the boil, then reduce the heat and simmer for 45 minutes, stirring occasionally.

Stir in the sugar and leave to simmer for a further 45 minutes, stirring occasionally.

Remove from the heat and let cool, then whizz the mixture in a food processor. You can leave it a little chunky if you like, or keep whizzing until it's smooth. Decant the ketchup into sterilized bottles or containers and seal or cover. Keep refrigerated for up to 3 weeks, or you can freeze it, if you like.

Sweet Chilli Sticky Sweetcorn

A lovely accompaniment to serve with a main course/entrée or with a salumi platter.

1 whole corn cob, leaves and 'silk' stripped off

20 g/generous 1 tablespoon butter

½ fresh red chilli/chile, deseeded and finely chopped (or use a pinch of dried chilli/hot pepper flakes)

2 teaspoons white wine vinegar

3 tablespoons demerara/raw sugar

a squeeze of fresh lime juice

SERVES 4

Cook the corn cob in a pan of boiling water for 10 minutes over medium heat until tender, then drain and cool slightly.

Melt the butter in a frying pan/skillet over medium heat and fry the chilli/chile on its own for 2 minutes. Add the vinegar, sugar and 2 tablespoons water, stir well and bring to the boil. Reduce the heat to a low simmer and cook until the mixture reduces and becomes sticky.

Meanwhile, using a sharp knife, carefully cut the corn kernels off the cob. Stir the corn kernels into the sticky mixture in the frying pan/skillet.

Remove from the heat and transfer the mixture to a dish. Leave to cool for at least 5 minutes before serving – be careful to let it cool sufficiently, because the sugar is caramelized and very hot.

This can also be served cold. Pop it into an airtight container and keep in the refrigerator for up to 3 days.

Warm Infused Olives

These olives are perfect to serve with any cured meats. Make sure you put some crusty bread with them too, so that guests can soak up the delicious oil.

3 tablespoons olive oil
1 garlic clove, finely chopped
¼ fresh red chilli/chile, deseeded and finely chopped
a pinch of ground ginger
a good squeeze of fresh lime juice
150–200 g/5–7 oz. unseasoned green or black olives
sea salt and freshly ground black pepper

SERVES 2

Start with about one-third of the olive oil in a frying pan/skillet, heat it over medium heat, then add the garlic, chilli/chile, ginger and lime juice, and fry until the garlic and chilli/chile pieces are brown and crispy. Add the rest of the olive oil and continue to fry until bubbling.

Reduce the heat right down to a simmer and throw in the olives. Stir for a few minutes to heat them through, making sure that the olives don't cook on the bottom of the frying pan/skillet.

Remove from the heat, add salt and pepper to taste, then transfer the mixture to a heatproof dish. Serve.

This mixture will keep in the refrigerator for up to 5 days; you might just have to warm it through again before serving to melt any oil that has set.

Sweet Patatas Bravas

Every time I go to a tapas restaurant with friends, we'll be going through the menu and then someone will say, 'Ooooh, patatas bravas, yes?', which is met with a chorus of 'patatas bravas', 'patatas bravas' – so I think that people enjoy saying it as much as they like eating it. I use sweet potatoes here, but you can use any type of potatoes you like.

FOR THE SAUCE

1 tablespoon olive oil
1 onion
1 garlic clove
1 teaspoon tomato purée/paste
2 teaspoons paprika
a pinch of dried chilli/hot
    pepper flakes
1 teaspoon soft/packed
    brown sugar
a big pinch of freshly chopped
    parsley, plus extra to garnish
a pinch of freshly chopped or
    dried basil
1 tablespoon red wine vinegar
400-g/14-oz. can of tomatoes,
    chopped
sea salt and freshly ground
    black pepper

FOR THE POTATOES

3 large sweet potatoes, cut
    roughly into cubes (I'm a big
    fan of keeping the peel on,
    but it's up to you)
2 tablespoons olive oil

SERVES 4

First, make the sauce. Ideally, make this the day before you want to serve it or follow the instructions to cool below.

Heat the olive oil in a frying pan/skillet over medium heat. Add the onion and fry it until soft and browning, then add the garlic and fry briefly. Add the tomato purée/paste, paprika, chilli/hot pepper flakes, sugar, parsley and basil , season with salt and pepper, and cook, stirring, for 1 minute. Add the vinegar and canned tomatoes, then reduce the heat and simmer for 5–6 minutes, until it thickens a little. Remove from the heat.

If you're making this the day before, let the mixture cool to room temperature, then place it in the refrigerator overnight (it will keep in an airtight container in the refrigerator for up to 3 days, or it can be frozen for another time). If you're making this sauce on the day you want to serve it, I strongly recommend cooling then reheating it before you pour it over the roasted potato pieces, because this really brings out the flavours. So, just fill a sink with cold water and lower the bottom of the pan into the water (or transfer the mixture to a bowl to lower into the water, to be even quicker) and keep stirring until the sauce is cool and thicker still. Set aside.

Preheat the oven to 180°C (350°F) Gas 4.

Put the potatoes in a pan, cover with cold water, bring to the boil and boil for 5 minutes to soften them. Drain well, then transfer them to a baking sheet and spread them out in a single layer. Drizzle the olive oil over the top and mix them around so they're well covered.

Roast in the preheated oven for 15–20 minutes and give them a shake halfway through. If you have peeled the potatoes they won't take as long to roast, so just reduce the cooking time a little.

While the potatoes are roasting, reheat the sauce by gently heating it in a saucepan on the hob/stovetop over low heat.

Remove the roasted potatoes from the oven and pop them into individual dishes to serve (or transfer to one large serving dish). Pour the reheated sauce over the potatoes. Serve immediately, garnished with extra parsley.

Wholemeal Crispbread

The crispbread is a lovely thing to have with charcuterie, particularly the pâtés and rillettes, which are wonderfully rich.

1 tablespoon sunflower oil
100 g/generous ¾ cup wholemeal/ whole-wheat flour
a pinch of baking powder
a pinch of salt

a large baking sheet, greased

MAKES 8

Pre-heat the oven to 180°C (350°F) Gas 4.

Mix all the ingredients in a bowl with 1 tablespoon water (add a touch more water if it feels really dry). Bring it together into a dough.

Place the dough onto a flour-dusted surface and roll it into a large, thin circle or rectangle, certainly no more than 5 mm/¼ inch thick.

Transfer the rolled dough to the prepared baking sheet, using the rolling pin to help you lift it. Score the surface into slices with a knife (like pizza slices or little rectangles). Try and go quite deep with this, and don't worry if you nick all the way through the crispbread.

Bake in the preheated oven for 20–25 minutes until crisp.

Remove from the oven and let cool until it is cool enough to touch, then carefully break it along the scored lines. The sooner you can do this the better, so don't let it go completely cold before you do it.

Home-baked Oatcakes

Yum, I love oatcakes. I would choose them over any other savoury biscuit/cracker in all the world, even if that decision was forever. I'm serious. Try me.

100 g/3¾ oz. rolled/porridge oats
50 g/scant ½ cup plain/all-purpose flour
40 g/3 tablespoons butter (at room temperature)
a pinch of baking powder
a pinch of sea salt
additions as you wish – see Cook's Note (optional)
milk, for brushing

4-cm/1½-inch round or square cookie cutter
a large baking sheet, greased

MAKES ABOUT 14

Preheat the oven to 180°C (350°F) Gas 4.

Put everything (except the milk for brushing) into a bowl and mix really well with your hands, crumbling the ingredients together. Add 2 tablespoons cold water, a little at a time, mixing with your hands, until you have a soft dough.

Place the dough onto a flour-dusted surface and roll it out to the thickness that you'd like. Use the cookie cutter to stamp out circles or squares and pop them on the prepared baking sheet, leaving a little space between each one. Brush a little milk over the top of each one.

Bake in the preheated oven on the middle shelf for 12–15 minutes. Transfer to a wire rack and let cool completely. Store in an airtight container for a week or two. You can freeze them for up to 6 months.

Cook's Note
You can mix all sorts of things into your oatcakes: herbs, dried fruit pieces, crushed roast (peeled) chestnuts, finely grated lime or lemon zest, or dried chilli/hot pepper flakes.

Crostino

Another traditional Italian bread
accompaniment made using ciabatta.

1 ciabatta loaf, thinly sliced
olive oil, to drizzle
sea salt and freshly ground black pepper

SERVES 4

Preheat the grill/broiler to medium.

Cut the ciabatta loaf into 1 cm/½ inch slices.

Drizzle some olive oil onto a large baking sheet
and then lay the ciabatta slices on top. Drizzle a little
more olive oil over the top of the slices, then sprinkle
with salt and pepper.

Grill/broil the slices for 4–5 minutes, turning
halfway through. Serve immediately.

Garlic-y Bruschetta

This is such an easy accompaniment for so
many charcuterie boards.

1 baguette
1 garlic clove, peeled
olive oil, to drizzle

SERVES 4

Preheat the grill/broiler to medium.

Slice the baguette diagonally into 1 cm/½ inch
slices. Rub the garlic clove around the edge of the
baguette slices – the hard crust will rub the flavour
off the garlic clove without overpowering the bread.

Drizzle oil onto a baking sheet and lay the slices
on top. Drizzle a little more olive oil over the tops.

Grill/broil for 4–5 minutes, turning halfway
through. Serve immediately.

Melba Toast

2 slices white or wholemeal/
    whole-wheat bread
sea salt and freshly ground
    black pepper

MAKES 16 PIECES

Preheat the grill/broiler to medium.

Cut the top crust off each slice of bread. Lightly toast the bread on both sides, either under the preheated grill/broiler or using a toaster on a low setting.

Remove from the grill/broiler or toaster and slice horizontally through the middle of each slice of toast to halve the thickness, then cut each slice diagonally both ways to make 4 triangles. You should now have 16 triangles.

Lay the triangles on a baking sheet with the untoasted sides facing up, sprinkle salt and pepper over the top and then pop them under the preheated grill/broiler for 1–2 minutes, until the tops are toasted. Serve immediately.

SMALL BITES

Salumi Chips (Baked Salumi)

So simple and yet so moreish. I've tried this with lots of different varieties of salumi and, as you'll see in the Mediterranean Pasta Bake recipe (see page 155), it's also a great addition to a main dish. This is a slightly leaner way to enjoy charcuterie too, as you'll see some of the fat drain out of it. I have to say that my personal favourite for this is saucisson sec, but feel free to try it with any slices of charcuterie, such as recipe-cured (salami, chorizo, etc, where the meat is minced/ground and mixed with flavourings) or straight-cured (prosciutto, for example, where whole joints of meat are cured).

12 slices salumi of your choice

MAKES 12

Preheat the oven to 180°C (350°F) Gas 4.

Lay the slices of salumi in a single layer on a baking sheet. Bake in the preheated oven for 20–25 minutes, until crisp. Keep checking that they're not burning. Remove from the oven and let cool.

Store in an airtight container in the refrigerator. These chips will last for up to a week in the refrigerator and are the perfect thing to nibble on.

Chorizo & Scallop Skewers

This is as lovely a combination of textures as it is of flavours. The scallops become slightly pink with the chorizo oil, and the taste of paprika permeates the soft flesh. I use these two ingredients together again in the Scallop, Chorizo, Chilli and Quinoa Stew (see page 171). I'm also a fan of frozen scallops. I find they cook beautifully and are great to have on stand-by. Given that chorizo has such a lovely long shelf-life, having a bag of frozen scallops means that this combination is on hand for all sorts of recipes – from canapés and stews to salads and risottos.

12 shelled scallops (or frozen
   scallops, defrosted)
12 x 1-cm/½-inch cubes chorizo
sea salt and freshly ground
   black or pink pepper
olive oil, for frying
paprika, for sprinkling

MAKES 12

First fry the scallops in a little olive oil in a frying pan/skillet over high heat for 1 minute on each side, until cooked. Add a good scrunch of pepper, then add the chorizo cubes and fry for a further 2–3 minutes, turning and stirring everything often.

Remove the chorizo and scallops from the pan, and leave until cool enough to handle, then thread one scallop and chorizo cube onto a cocktail stick/toothpick. I recommend putting the scallop on first as the chorizo does a better job of gripping the stick.

Repeat to make 12 canapés in total. Serve immediately, while still warm, sprinkled with a little paprika, if you like.

Variation
You can always add a little chilli/chili powder or paprika to coat the scallops before cooking, but I find that enough flavourful oil comes out of good-quality chorizo as you fry it.

'Sushi-style' Prosciutto-wrapped Goat's Cheese & Rocket

Sushi was another triumph in man's battle against shelf-life. Like salumi, the method of fermenting fish with rice and vinegars was designed to extend the life of the fish. Before methods were developed to make the rice and wrapping just as delicious as the fish in the middle, the rice was discarded before the fish was eaten. So, as a tribute to our ancestors' peers in the Far East, here's a sushi-inspired recipe using charcuterie.

12 slices prosciutto

3 tablespoons Puttanesca Relish
(see page 62)

a handful of rocket/arugula
(about 4–5 leaves per roll)

200 g/7 oz. goat's cheese, sliced
into 12 strips (or cheese of your
choice; Gorgonzola is good too)

MAKES 24

Lay a slice of prosciutto flat on a board or plate. Spread 1 teaspoon of the relish over the surface. Sprinkle 4–5 rocket/arugula leaves on the top, then put a strip of cheese on top in the middle.

Roll the prosciutto over on itself to enclose the filling, like a 'nori roll', and then slice (it is easiest to snip with kitchen scissors) in half to create two circles. Push a cocktail stick/toothpick through each assembled bite to hold it together.

Repeat to make 24 bites in total. Serve immediately.

Alternatively, roll each slice of prosciutto with its filling into a cone so it's wider at the top, like 'temaki'. You will make 12 larger bites using this method.

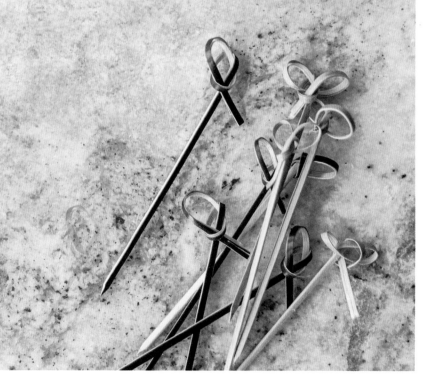

Cornichons Wrapped in Salami

As simple as the name suggests. These mini gherkins are often served with salami because the flavours complement each other perfectly. This combination really is a delight for the tastebuds – saltiness from the meat and acidity of the pickled cornichons. If you put them side by side on the plate, nobody can resist rolling them up, so you might as well do the work for them!

12 slices salami
12 cornichons (or 12 small slices
   of pickled gherkin)
freshly ground black pepper

MAKES 12

For each bite, just wrap a slice of salami around a cornichon and pop a cocktail stick/toothpick through the middle to hold them together. Easy, right? I assure you, I spent only a proportionate amount of time on this recipe…

Repeat to make 12 bites in total. Crack a little pepper over the plate and serve.

Mozzarella Pearls Wrapped in Prosciutto

So simple, just like the recipe above. Don't use a whole slice of prosciutto per mini mozzarella pearl/ball, as that's a heavy mouthful, as well as being expensive for entertaining. I use kitchen scissors to cut each slice of prosciutto into quarters.

3 slices prosciutto
12 mini mozzarella pearls/balls
freshly ground black pepper

MAKES 12

Cut each slice of prosciutto lengthways in quarters (kitchen scissors are best for doing this) to make 12 strips in total. Wrap each strip around a mini mozzarella pearl/ball.

Pop a cocktail stick/toothpick through the middle of each assembled bite to hold it together, crack a little black pepper over the plate and serve.

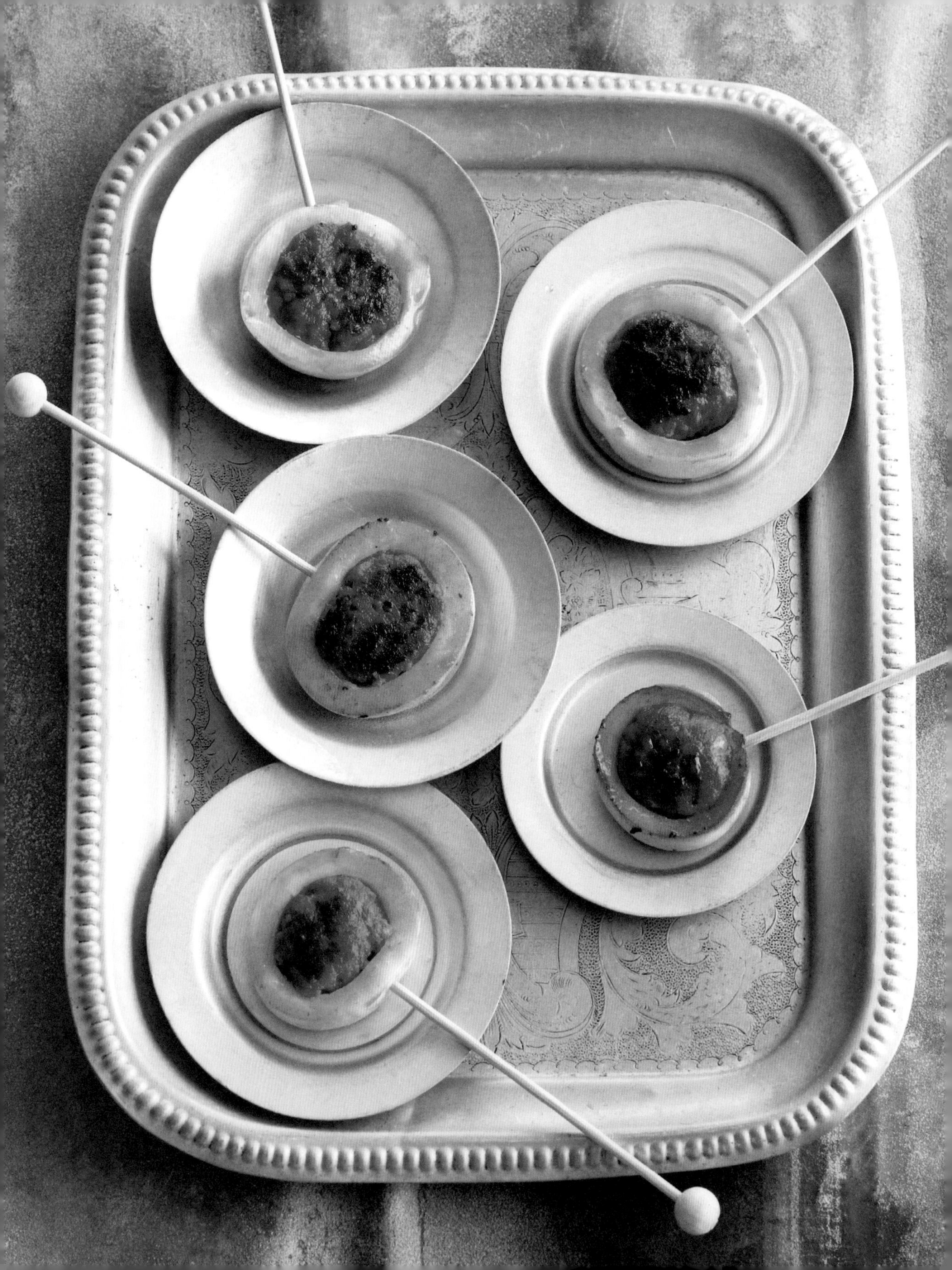

Chorizo & Calamari 'Planets'

This is another recipe for a cocktail stick/toothpick canapé, but you lay them flat, like a chicken satay, for example. These are really simple and quick to do, especially if you use pre-cooked calamari. I think they look like planets, hence the name!

12 rings calamari/raw squid
  (or use cooked calamari)
12 x 1-cm/½-inch cubes chorizo
olive oil, for frying

MAKES 12

Heat a non-stick frying pan/skillet over medium heat. If you're using raw squid, place it in the hot pan with a little olive oil, and cook for about 8 minutes, until the rings have firmed up. Remove from the pan and allow to cool slightly.

Push a cube of chorizo into the middle of a calamari ring, then secure it in place with a cocktail stick/toothpick, pushing the cocktail stick/toothpick through the side of the calamari ring, through the chorizo in the middle and out the other side of the calamari ring. Repeat to make 12 canapés in total.

Lay the prepared canapés back in the hot frying pan/skillet and cook over medium heat for 2–3 minutes, until the chorizo starts to warm and soften and the oil produced from the chorizo coats the calamari. Serve immediately.

Devils on Horseback

There's a debate about when these bites had their 'heyday', which only means they've never gone away. So, let's keep the Devils on Horseback alive and cantering, and put a charcuterie spin on it!

6 slices prosciutto
12 whole blanched almonds
12 pitted dried dates or prunes

MAKES 12

Cut each slice of prosciutto lengthways down the middle (kitchen scissors work best for doing this) to make 12 half-slices.

For each 'devil', put an almond in the middle of a pitted date, wrap a half slice of prosciutto tightly around the fruit and then lay it on a baking sheet. Repeat to make 12 'devils' in total.

Preheat the grill/broiler to high.

Grill/broil the 'devils' for about 5 minutes, until the prosciutto starts to brown and crisp. Turn the 'devils' over and grill/broil for a further 2–3 minutes. Push a cocktail stick/toothpick through the middle of each one and serve immediately.

Horses on Devilback

Huh? Horses on Devilback? Yes, fair's fair. It's the horse's turn now. I've recommended using saucisson sec or Serrano ham here because of their dark, rich flavour.

12 pitted prunes
12 slices saucisson sec or 6 slices
 Serrano ham
6 teaspoons mango chutney

MAKES 12

Make sure that the pitted prunes each have a hole that goes all the way through the middle. If you are using Serrano ham, cut each slice lengthways down the middle using scissors to make 12 half-slices.

For each 'horse', take a slice of saucisson sec or a half-slice of Serrano ham. Spread ½ teaspoon mango chutney over each slice of meat, then roll the meat into a tight tube, and thread it through the middle of a prune. Lay it on a baking sheet. Repeat to make 12 'horses' in total.

Preheat the grill/broiler to high.

Grill/broil the 'horses' for a about 2 minutes to warm them through, turning once. Push a cocktail stick/toothpick through the middle of each one and serve immediately.

Angels on Horseback

The mango chutney is optional here, but I like it because it adds sweetness to the salty first taste and softens the smokiness of the oysters. These are always a party favourite!

6 slices prosciutto
6 teaspoons mango chutney (optional)
12 smoked oysters

MAKES 12

Cut each slice of prosciutto lengthways down the middle to make 12 half-slices in total.

Spread ½ teaspoon mango chutney at one end of a half-slice of prosciutto. Place a smoked oyster on top and roll up the prosciutto around the oyster. Repeat to make 12 'angels' in total.

Heat a non-stick frying pan/skillet over medium heat until hot. Add the 'angels' to the pan. Cook them over medium heat for 1 minute, then turn over and cook for 1 minute more. This is merely to warm them through and release the flavour of the prosciutto.

Push a cocktail stick/toothpick through the middle of each one and serve immediately.

Pizzettes

These are mini pizzas. They're quite filling, so they're ideal for a drinks party when you have no intention of keeping your guests for dinner. Or they can be an appetizer if your main course/entrée isn't too heavy. They are also useful for lunch menus if you serve two together or make slightly larger ones, and make great children's party food.

FOR THE BASE/CRUST

170 g/1½ cups plain/all-purpose
   or wholemeal/whole-wheat flour
a small pinch of fast-action/
   rapid-rise yeast
1 tablespoon olive oil
a pinch of sea salt
1 teaspoon caster/granulated
   sugar

FOR THE TOPPING

1 tablespoon olive oil
300 g/11 oz. pancetta, thinly sliced
   or diced
400-g/14-oz. can of tomatoes,
   drained and chopped
a big pinch of freshly chopped
   parsley
a big pinch of freshly chopped
   or dried oregano
1 tablespoon tomato purée/paste
about 40 g/1½ oz. Caramelized
   Red Onions (see page 61)
   (optional)
200 g/7 oz. pecorino or Parmesan
   cheese, grated or shaved
sea salt and freshly ground
   black pepper

*a large baking sheet, greased
   or lined with parchment paper*

MAKES 6 PIZZETTES

Preheat the oven to 180°C (350°F) Gas 4.

For the base/crust, put all the ingredients in a bowl, add 125 ml/½ cup water and mix together with your hands to make a dough. If the mixture feels sloppy, just add a little more flour, or add a little more water for the opposite (it shouldn't be so dry that it crumbles when you roll it). Turn the dough out onto a flour-dusted surface and knead for 5–10 minutes, until smooth and elastic. The kneading is always a bit boring but just remember that you need (groan!) to do it or your base will be chewy and tough. If you have a bread maker, it will do the work for you – just follow the timing instructions for your machine.

Divide the dough into six even pieces. On a flour-dusted surface, roll out each portion of dough into an oval. Place the pizza bases/crusts on the prepared baking sheet and bake in the preheated oven for 10 minutes, turning over halfway through.

Meanwhile, prepare the topping. Heat the olive oil in a frying pan/skillet. Add the pancetta and fry over medium heat, until fully cooked – let it brown but don't reduce it right down at this stage because it will continue to bake on top of the pizzettes. Put the canned tomatoes, parsley, oregano and tomato purée/paste into a bowl, season with salt and pepper, and mix well.

Once the pizza bases/crusts are initially baked, remove from the oven. Spread the tomato mixture over the top of the bases/crusts and then spoon over the caramelized onions, if using. Put the pancetta pieces on top, then sprinkle over the cheese.

Return the pizzettes to the preheated oven on the middle shelf (ideally, put the pizzettes directly onto the oven shelf, rather than using the baking sheet, so the bases can continue to crisp) and bake for a further 15 minutes, until the cheese has melted. Serve hot.

'Scotch Eggs'

This is a take on traditional Scotch eggs for a little canapé.
It's a very easy version to prepare too.

12 quail's eggs
6 slices prosciutto, coppa
   or Serrano ham
sea salt and freshly ground
   black pepper

MAKES 12

Hard-boil/hard-cook the quail's eggs in a pan of boiling water for 5 minutes. Drain and plunge the eggs into cold water, then drain again and let cool. Remove the shells, dry the eggs with paper towels and then roll them in salt and freshly ground black pepper.

Cut each slice of cured ham lengthways down the middle (kitchen scissors are easiest for doing this) to make 12 half-slices in total.

Roll each quail's egg up inside a half-slice of ham. You might need to insert a cocktail stick/toothpick through each canapé if the quail's eggs are bigger, but they'll hold together by themselves if they're small. Serve immediately.

Millionaire's Finger Food

This is one of the more unusual conversation-starters at a drinks party: "Do you know, that mouthful costs more per kg/lb than 9-carat gold...!"

The process of making charcuterie is long and very expensive. Jamón Ibérico de Bellota takes more than four years to produce and has pigs roaming around forests getting fat on acorns. This particular example is one of the most expensive foods (let alone meats) that one can buy.

So, if you fold some of that on a cocktail stick/toothpick with a small spoonful of black truffle pâté (foie gras is even slightly more expensive, but I confidently denounce the process), and serve with a little pot of mayonnaise seasoned with saffron and lime, you have a very valuable mouthful indeed. You would need only a tiny amount of saffron and a small piece of the ham and the truffle pâté but still, it's a pretty swanky way to start a drinks party, isn't it?

12 small strips jamón Ibérico
3 teaspoons black truffle pâté

FOR THE SAFFRON MAYONNAISE
4 tablespoons good-quality
  mayonnaise
a pinch of saffron (about
  8 strands)
a squeeze of fresh lime juice
sea salt and freshly ground
  black pepper

MAKES 12

To make each one of these tasty morsels, wrap a small strip of jamón Ibérico around ¼ teaspoon black truffle pâté. Repeat to make 12 tasty morsels in total.

Put a cocktail stick/toothpick through the middle of each one to hold the ham in place. Alternatively, for elegant presentation, use dainty little forks instead.

These are delicious dipped into saffron mayonnaise. It is quick and easy to make – mix the mayonnaise with the saffron and a squeeze of lime juice, then season to taste with salt and pepper.

Cured Duck & Mustard Bruschetta

If you can't find cured duck breast, you could use slices of any cured meats.
I'd recommend a good, rich cured meat – cured mutton is ideal if you can buy it,
or cured venison is delicious and very lean.

4 slices Garlic-y Bruschetta
   (see page 72)
about 2 teaspoons wholegrain
   mustard (Dijon/French or
   English/ hot mustard also
   work well)
a handful of rocket/arugula leaves
12 slices cured duck breast

MAKES 4

Spread some mustard on each slice of bruschetta. Arrange
a few leaves of rocket/arugula on the top and layer the slices
of cured meat over the top. Serve immediately.

If your bruschetta slice is larger than bite-size, or if you're
not eating it with a knife and fork, I recommend cutting each
slice of cured meat into 2 or 3 smaller pieces. This is just
because if you pick it up and bite it, you'll probably pull the
whole slice of meat off with the first mouthful and the rest
of your bruschetta will never be the same!

Chicken Liver Pâté

I have no idea why I grew up thinking that pâté was hard to make. It isn't. Even the hardened butter on the top used to look like a secret trick to perfect. It's not. The foundation of a simple chicken liver pâté can also be a great basis for some fun with additional flavours and ingredients. Here's a classic combination to get you started.

45 g/3½ tablespoons butter

2 shallots, chopped

1 garlic clove, chopped

75 g/3 oz. pork belly
    (rind removed), diced

200 g/7 oz. chicken livers, chopped

a pinch of freshly chopped thyme,
    plus extra to decorate

1 tablespoon brandy

2 bay leaves

a squeeze of fresh lemon juice
    (about 1 teaspoon)

sea salt and freshly ground
    black pepper

black and pink peppercorns,
    to decorate

Wholemeal Crispbread
    (see page 70) or Home-baked
    Oatcakes (see page 70),
    to serve

SERVES 4

Heat 20 g/generous 1 tablespoon of the butter in a frying pan/skillet over medium heat, until melted. Add the shallots and garlic and fry on their own for 1 minute. Add the pork belly, chicken livers, thyme and brandy, season with salt and pepper, and stir. Put the bay leaves on top and let them soften, if you are using dried ones. Cook, stirring regularly for 10 minutes, until everything is browned and the chicken livers are cooked through.

Remove from the heat and let cool until the mixture is warm, not hot – don't let it cool completely, otherwise the ingredients will dry out. Remove and discard the bay leaves.

Put the mixture into a food processor (don't wash the pan yet), add a squeeze of lemon juice and whizz. It's up to you how coarse you like it. I like a quite smooth pâté, so I process until the mixture sticks to the sides. You can also pulse for a short time and keep some chunks, if you prefer. Spoon the mixture into a dish (or into separate ramekins) and level the surface so that the melted butter can go on top.

In the same frying pan/skillet you were using before, melt the remaining butter over medium heat, until it starts to bubble, and then remove from the heat and pour over the top of the pâté. Decorate with a little extra thyme and some black and pink peppercorns. Move the pâté to the refrigerator and the butter will set in about 1 hour.

Serve with Wholemeal Crispbread or Home-baked Oatcakes.

The pâté will keep in the refrigerator for 1 week, if the butter is unbroken on the top. Eat within 3 days once you have dipped through the surface. You can freeze the pâté in balls wrapped in clingfilm/plastic wrap (without the melted butter topping) and slowly defrost (do not reheat nor microwave). Once defrosted, you can transfer to ramekins and add the melted butter to the top.

Pâté with Dried Apricots & Pistachios

In this recipe, I have had a bit of fun with a classic pâté, and the results are delicious. The sweetness from the apricots is lovely alongside the richness of the chicken livers, and the texture, with the pistachio nuts, is really pleasing if you keep it chunky.

45 g/3½ tablespoons butter
½ red onion, chopped
½ garlic clove, chopped
75 g/3 oz. pork belly (rind removed), diced
200 g/7 oz. chicken livers, chopped
1 tablespoon brandy or Cointreau
60 g/2½ oz. ready-to-eat dried apricots, chopped
15 g/½ oz. shelled pistachio nuts
a squeeze of fresh lemon juice (about 1 teaspoon)
sea salt and freshly ground black pepper
finely sliced ready-to-eat dried apricots and pistachios, to decorate
Home-baked Oatcakes (see page 70) or Wholemeal Crispbread (see page 70), to serve

SERVES 4

Heat 20 g/generous 1 tablespoon of the butter in a frying pan/skillet over medium heat until melted. Add the red onion and garlic, and fry on their own for 1 minute. Add the pork belly, chicken livers and brandy, season with salt and pepper, and stir. Cook, stirring regularly for 10 minutes, until everything is browned and the pork belly and chicken livers are cooked through.

Remove from the heat and let cool until the mixture is warm, not hot – don't let it cool completely, otherwise the ingredients will dry out.

Put the mixture into a food processor (don't wash the pan yet), add the apricots, pistachio nuts and the squeeze of lemon juice, and whizz. I like to keep this mixture chunky so that you still get a bite of apricot and the soft crunch of pistachio in the pâté. However, you can blitz until smooth, if you prefer. Spoon the mixture into a dish (or into separate ramekins) and level the surface so that the melted butter can go on top.

In the same frying pan/skillet you were using before, melt the remaining butter over medium heat, until it starts to bubble, and then remove from the heat and pour over the top of the pâté. Decorate with slices of dried apricot and pistachios. Move the pâté to the refrigerator and the butter will set in about 1 hour.

Serve with Home-baked Oatcakes or Wholemeal Crispbread.

The pâté will keep in the refrigerator for 1 week, if the butter is unbroken on the top. Eat within 3 days once you have dipped through the surface. You can freeze the pâté in balls wrapped in clingfilm/plastic wrap (without the melted butter topping) and slowly defrost (do not reheat nor microwave). Once defrosted, you can transfer to ramekins and add the melted butter to the top.

Dried Cranberry & Brandy Christmas Pâté

A Christmas-themed pâté to serve at a seasonal gathering – or to keep in the refrigerator and nibble on at intervals, which is allowed at Christmastime, of course.

45 g/3½ tablespoons butter
2 shallots, chopped
1 garlic clove, chopped
2 tablespoons brandy
75 g/3 oz. pork belly (rind removed), diced
150 g/5 oz. chicken livers, chopped
a pinch of ground cloves
50 g/2 oz. dried cranberries, chopped, plus extra to decorate
a squeeze of fresh lemon juice (about 1 teaspoon)
sea salt and freshly ground black pepper
Melba Toast, to serve (see page 73)

SERVES 4

Heat 20 g/generous 1 tablespoon of the butter in a frying pan/skillet over medium heat until melted. Add the shallots and garlic, and fry on their own for 1 minute. Add the brandy and cook for 1 minute, then add the pork belly, chicken livers and cloves, season with salt and pepper, and stir. Cook, stirring regularly for 10 minutes, until everything is browned and the pork belly and chicken livers are cooked through.

Remove from the heat and let cool until the mixture is warm, not hot – don't let it cool completely, otherwise the ingredients will dry out.

Put the mixture into a food processor (don't wash the pan yet), add the cranberries and the squeeze of lemon juice, and whizz. It's up to you how coarse you like it. I like quite a smooth pâté so I process until the mixture sticks to the sides. You can also pulse for a short time and keep some chunks, if you prefer. Spoon the mixture into a dish (or into separate ramekins) and level the surface so that the melted butter can go on top.

In the same frying pan/skillet you were using before, melt the remaining butter over medium heat, until it starts to bubble, and then remove from the heat and pour over the top of the pâté. Decorate with dried cranberries. Move the pâté to the refrigerator and the butter will set in about 1 hour.

Serve with Melba Toast.

The pâté will keep in the refrigerator for 1 week, if the butter is unbroken on the top. Eat within 3 days once you have dipped through the surface. You can freeze the pâté in balls wrapped in clingfilm/plastic wrap (without the melted butter topping) and slowly defrost (do not reheat nor microwave). Once defrosted, you can transfer to ramekins and add the melted butter to the top.

Pâté de Campagne

This is not technically a pâté, but is similar to the Pork Rillettes on page 105, in that it is served like one. This recipe needs to be made the day before serving.

30 g/2 tablespoons butter

2 tablespoons brandy

4 shallots, finely chopped

1 garlic clove, finely chopped

1 egg

4 tablespoons double/heavy cream

½ teaspoon Dijon mustard

a pinch of fresh thyme leaves

400 g/14 oz. pork loin or shoulder (as much fat removed as possible), trimmed and cut into 1-cm/½-inch dice

6 slices prosciutto

100 g/3½ oz. ham hock, chopped (optional)

hard-boiled egg, peeled (optional)

sea salt and freshly ground black pepper

20 x 10-cm/8 x 4-inch loaf pan, greased

SERVES 4/MAKES 1 LOAF

Preheat the oven to 180°C (350°F) Gas 4.

Melt the butter in a frying pan/skillet over medium heat, then add the brandy. Let it boil and reduce for a minute, then add the shallots and garlic. Once those have softened, remove the frying pan/skillet from the heat and let cool.

In a bowl, beat the egg and then stir in the cream, mustard and thyme, and season with salt and pepper. Add the diced pork, then stir in the cooled shallot mixture and any juices from the pan.

Lay the slices of prosciutto across the bottom and up the sides of the prepared loaf pan so that they line the pan. I recommend leaving just a small gap between the slices so that the loaf is easier to slice once it's cooked and then chilled. Spoon half of the pork mixture into the pan and then sprinkle the ham hock pieces across the middle, if using. You can have a bit of fun here by placing a peeled hard-boiled egg in the middle. It looks attractive when sliced.

Spoon the remaining pork mixture on top and then fold in the ends of the prosciutto, if the slices are longer than the inside surface of the loaf pan. Cover the pan tightly with foil. Take a larger roasting dish and put 2.5 cm/1 inch of water in the bottom. Lower the loaf pan into the water and cook in the preheated oven for 1 hour, until the mixture around the meat has thickened and the meat is firm to the touch. Remove the loaf pan from the water bath and let cool for 30 minutes.

The loaf pan should now be cool enough to move to the refrigerator to finish setting. The pâté will take a good few hours to set properly, which is why I recommend making it the day before.

Like with the Pork Rillettes recipe, I wouldn't serve this straight from the refrigerator. I let it come to room temperature for about 20–30 minutes before serving.

When it comes to serving, just run a knife around the edge of the loaf to release it from the sides of the pan and then turn it out onto a board. You'll now see what I mean about leaving the small gap between the prosciutto so that you can slice the softer mixture below it without dragging the prosciutto with your knife.

This pâté is heavenly served with an ice-cold glass of dry white wine like Sancerre and maybe a game of pétanque in a French courtyard!

Pork Rillettes

Rillettes are like a pâté with a bit more texture, because the meat is shredded, rather than puréed. Best served at room temperature, with some Melba toast or crispbread, this is a special and flavourful appetizer or canapé, and very easy to make.

200 g/7 oz. pork belly (rindless), trimmed and diced
1 tablespoon sea salt
30 g/2 tablespoons butter
1 garlic clove, finely chopped
a small pinch of ground mace
1 bay leaf
a pinch of freshly chopped or dried parsley
50 ml/scant ¼ cup dry white wine
150 ml/⅔ cup chicken stock
sea salt and freshly ground black pepper
freshly squeezed lemon juice and freshly chopped parsley, to serve (optional)
Melba Toast, to serve (see page 73)

SERVES 2

Put the pork belly in a non-metallic container and sprinkle the salt over the top. Massage the salt into the meat, then cover tightly and refrigerate for 1–2 hours. Rinse and dry the pork cubes – the salt should have already drawn some of the moisture out of the pork belly, but you don't want to draw out too much because you're going to slow-cook it, which will benefit from keeping the fat.

Melt the butter in a saucepan over medium heat (you're going to need a saucepan with a lid), then add the pork belly, garlic, mace, bay leaf and parsley, and season with salt and pepper. Cook, stirring often, to slightly brown the pork and coat it in the seasoning, then add the white wine and keep increase the heat to high for 1–2 minutes to reduce the wine. Pour in the chicken stock.

Turn the heat down to very low and put the lid on the pan. Leave it cooking gently for 1¼ hours. At this stage, press one of the cubes of pork with a fork and if it starts to fall apart, it's had long enough. However, it's likely that it'll need a little longer. If the mixture is starting to dry out and stick to the bottom of the pan, just add another splash of chicken stock – about 50 ml/scant ¼ cup. Replace the lid and leave to cook gently for another 20–30 minutes, until the meat is falling apart.

Remove from the heat and leave to cool. Discard the bay leaf.

The best way to shred the pork is with your fingers, so let it cool enough to touch, then pull it apart with your fingers and mix it really well. If you have a large piece of fat on its own, you can remove it, but the fat should have mostly melted.

Transfer the pork to a container or 2 ramekins and chill in the refrigerator for at least 1 hour so that the mixture can set.

I recommend bringing it out of the refrigerator about 30 minutes before serving – the texture of shredded meat is best at room temperature and it allows the flavour to come through really well. Feel free to add a squeeze of lemon juice before serving, an extra crack of black pepper and a sprinkling of freshly chopped parsley, if you like.

Cook's Note
This recipe uses pork belly but the same process works well with duck.

PLATES, SALADS & SANDWICHES

Parma Ham & Melon Plate with Fresh Lime

This is such a classic appetizer and what it lacks in imagination and flair, it gains in everyone still having plenty of room for a lovely big main course/entrée. So don't knock it until you've had seconds of dessert, when you'll thank it. I've a take on it though, which I prefer to melon. Traditional recipe first, alternative on page 110.

8 slices Parma ham

½ melon, peeled, deseeded and sliced into thin slices

4 squeezes of fresh lime juice and finely grated zest to finish

4 pinches of freshly ground black pepper

SERVES 4

Divide the ham and melon evenly between the serving plates. Either place the Parma ham and melon neatly on the plate next to each other or wrap the Parma ham around the slices of melon. Squeeze lime juice over the top of each serving and sprinkle with a little finely grated lime zest. Finish with a generous amount of freshly ground black pepper.

Parma Ham & Grapefruit Plate
with Sloe Gin

With this alternative recipe, I recommend serving the grapefruit segments and Parma ham next to each other, rather than wrapping the Parma ham around the grapefruit. I only say this because I find tastebuds need to prepare themselves for grapefruit, even sweetened grapefruit like this. Your companions will instinctively put the right balance of the sour and salty on their fork to suit their own tastebuds. We do this the whole time, we don't even realise it.

8 white grapefruit segments
8 pink grapefruit segments
8 tablespoons sloe gin
   (or other fruit liqueur)
8 slices Parma ham

SERVES 4

Put the grapefruit segments into a bowl, pour over the sloe gin and leave to soak for at least 1 hour, but ideally for 3–4 hours. Serve with the Parma ham, allowing 4 grapefruit segments (plus some sloe gin) and 2 slices of Parma ham per serving.

Bresaola, Oven Tomatoes & Buffalo Mozzarella salad with Mustard Dressing

Bresaola is probably the best-known cured beef and I think it's a lovely way to enjoy beef. For many recipes, it combines even better with other flavours and ingredients than does cured pork, particularly in salads; it's generally a bit lighter in flavour and texture, so it works with the other ingredients rather than dominates them.

FOR THE SALAD

16–20 baby plum tomatoes, halved

1 tablespoon olive oil

a small bunch of fresh basil leaves (you want about 5–6 leaves per serving)

4 large handfuls of salad leaves/ greens of your choice – I recommend a mixture of baby leaf spinach and rocket/arugula

165 g/5½ oz. buffalo mozzarella, drained and torn into pieces (or use 32–36 mini mozzarella pearls/balls)

165 g/5½ oz. bresaola slices (about 20 average slices)

sea salt and freshly ground black pepper

FOR THE MUSTARD DRESSING

2 tablespoons olive oil

2 tablespoons balsamic vinegar

1 tablespoon runny honey

1 teaspoon wholegrain mustard

SERVES 4

For the salad, first make the oven tomatoes. These tomatoes are best if made a day before, or at least given time to chill down in the refrigerator, so they become chewier and absorb the oil.

Preheat the oven to 180°C (350°F) Gas 4.

Put the halved tomatoes in a shallow ovenproof dish and drizzle the olive oil over the top. Tear the basil leaves over the tomatoes, then season with salt and pepper. Roast in the preheated oven for about 15–20 minutes, giving them a shimmy halfway through. Remove from the oven and let cool, then refrigerate.

When you are ready to serve, make the mustard dressing by simply combining the olive oil, vinegar, honey and mustard in a bowl, seasoning with salt and pepper, and mixing well.

Dress the salad leaves/greens with most of the dressing (reserving a little dressing for drizzling on top) and divide between 4 serving plates, then pop the torn mozzarella (or 8–9 mini mozzarella pearls/balls per serving), chilled oven tomatoes and bresaola slices (see Cook's Note) on top, dividing them evenly between each plate. Drizzle the salads with the remaining dressing so that you get a taste of it even with the first mouthful, and serve immediately.

Cook's Note

It's always a shame to tear cured meat on top of salads, because it doesn't look as pretty. However, remember that cured meat like bresaola doesn't cut very easily, so if someone is just using a fork to eat the salad, they're only going to get 5 big mouthfuls of bresaola and then no more. Therefore, for the price of a little presentation, I would tear the bresaola into smaller pieces so it's distributed evenly for every mouthful.

Pancetta, Brussels Sprout, Chestnut & Camembert Salad
with Cranberry & Port Sauce

It's a good idea to schedule at least one salad into the Festive season menu... but that doesn't mean it has to be a flimsy salad. Why not combine lots of the classic Christmas flavours or leftovers in a delicious salad?

125 g/4¼ oz. pancetta, finely diced
4 handfuls of Brussels sprouts
    (about 165 g/5½ oz. in total),
    trimmed and halved
60 g/4 tablespoons butter
12–16 roasted chestnuts, peeled
    (see Cook's Note)
125 g/4¼ oz. Camembert, torn
    into pieces
sea salt and freshly ground
    black pepper
Romano lettuce leaves (or another
    soft leaf, like lollo rosso) and
    Cranberry and Port Sauce
    (see page 64), to serve, or
    storebought cranberry jelly
    is fine here too
olive oil, to drizzle

SERVES 4

Start by frying the pancetta in a hot frying pan/skillet until it's crisp and browned. Remove from the pan to a plate, but don't worry about washing up the frying pan/skillet just yet.

At the same time, steam (or boil) the Brussels sprouts over (or in) a separate pan of boiling water for 5 minutes until they soften. Drain and set aside.

Once you've removed the pancetta from the frying pan/skillet, add the butter to melt (and mix with the oils from the pancetta), then add the Brussels sprouts and chestnuts and mix well to coat in the buttery juices. Remove from the heat and season with salt and pepper.

For each serving, lay some lettuce leaves in each serving bowl, then put everything on top (pancetta, Brussels sprouts and chestnuts, and finally the Camembert), dividing the ingredients evenly between the bowls. Add a dollop of cranberry sauce on top of each portion and a drizzle of olive oil to dress. Crunch plenty of black pepper over the top and serve immediately.

Cook's Note
You can roast your own chestnuts for this recipe, or use ready-roasted.

Prosciutto, Artichoke, Fig & Roquefort Salad with Balsamic Dressing

A lovely, light summer salad – sweetness in the fig, saltiness in the prosciutto, and creamy Roquefort. A really simple balsamic dressing is fine for this one too, as there are already plenty of flavours in the salad.

FOR THE SALAD
60 g/4 tablespoons butter
4 fresh figs (skin on), quartered
4 large handfuls of salad leaves/
 greens of your choice (Little
 Gem/Bibb lettuce is very good
 for this salad)
125 g/4¼ oz. Roquefort cheese,
 crumbled
16–20 cooked artichoke hearts,
 chopped (I use the marinated
 artichoke hearts sold in jars)
165 g/5½ oz. prosciutto slices
 (about 20 average slices)
a small bunch of fresh basil leaves
 (about 5–6 leaves per serving)
sea salt and freshly ground
 black pepper

FOR THE DRESSING
2 tablespoons olive oil
1 tablespoon balsamic vinegar

SERVES 4

Preheat the grill/broiler to high.

For the salad, rub a little butter on all the cut surfaces of the figs, put them on a baking sheet, cut-sides up, and then pop them under the preheated grill/broiler for 6–8 minutes, turning once. Let them soften and start to brown, but don't let them shrivel up too much. Remove from the heat.

Meanwhile, make the dressing by combining the olive oil and vinegar in a bowl, seasoning with salt and pepper, and mixing well.

Dress the salad leaves/greens with most of the dressing (reserving a little dressing for drizzling on top) and divide between 4 serving plates, then pop the Roquefort, grilled figs, artichokes, prosciutto slices (see Cook's Note) and basil leaves on top, dividing them evenly between each plate. Drizzle the salads with the remaining dressing and serve immediately.

Cook's Note
Like with the Bresaola, Oven Tomatoes and Buffalo Mozzarella Salad with Mustard Dressing on page 113, it's always a shame to tear cured meat on top of salads because it doesn't look very pretty. However, remember that cured meat like prosciutto doesn't cut very easily, so if someone is just using a fork to eat the salad, they're only going to get 5 big mouthfuls of prosciutto and then no more. Therefore, for the price of a little presentation, I would tear the bresaola into smaller pieces so it's distributed evenly for every mouthful.

Broad Bean, Pea, Mint, Goat's Cheese & Fried Pancetta Salad

There is only one taste experience that can equal squeezing broad/fava beans fresh from the pod straight into your mouth... and that's making them all warm and buttery and mixing them with pancetta. This recipe is all about the freshness of flavour in broad/ fava beans, peas and mint, and mixing them with the richness of goat's cheese and pancetta to turn this from a side salad into a light meal.

125 g/4¼ oz. pancetta, finely diced
400 g/14 oz. broad/fava beans, shelled
200 g/scant 2 cups fresh or frozen peas
60 g/4 tablespoons butter
2 garlic cloves, finely chopped
a small handful of fresh mint leaves (about 12–16 leaves), chopped
1 tablespoon freshly chopped parsley
freshly squeezed juice of ½ lemon
125 g/4¼ oz. soft goat's cheese, torn into chunks
sea salt and freshly ground black pepper

SERVES 4

Start by frying the pancetta in a hot frying pan/skillet until it's crisp and browned. Remove from the pan to a plate, but don't worry about washing up the frying pan/skillet just yet.

At the same time, steam (or boil) the broad/fava beans and peas over (or in) a separate pan of boiling water for 4 minutes, until the broad/fava beans soften. Drain and set aside.

Once you've removed the pancetta from the pan, add the butter to melt (and mix with the oils from the pancetta), then add the garlic and allow that to brown, stirring often. Add the broad/fava beans, peas, mint, parsley, lemon juice and a pinch of salt, and mix well.

Remove from the heat and transfer to a salad bowl. Put the goat's cheese and pancetta on top. Crunch plenty of black pepper over and serve immediately.

Chorizo & Red Cabbage Salad

This salad is stunning due to its vibrant red colour. It's a lovely way to make cabbage exciting, as just a small amount of chorizo lends superb depth of flavour.

FOR THE SALAD

1 tablespoon olive oil

½ red cabbage, cored and sliced
   or shredded

150 g/5 oz. chorizo, peeled
   and diced

FOR THE DRESSING

3 tablespoons olive oil

1 tablespoon red wine vinegar

½ teaspoon garlic purée or
   crushed garlic

a big pinch of freshly chopped
   parsley

a pinch of freshly chopped
   or dried tarragon

1 teaspoon freshly squeezed
   lime juice

**SERVES 2 FOR
A LIGHT LUNCH**

For the salad, heat the olive oil in a frying pan/skillet over medium heat, then add the red cabbage and fry until soft, stirring regularly. Add the chorizo and keep stirring for 2–3 minutes, so that the chorizo starts to cook and releases its oils.

Remove from the heat and let cool.

Meanwhile, put all the ingredients for the dressing into a bowl and mix together well.

Once the cabbage and chorizo mixture has cooled, pour over the dressing, toss to mix, and serve.

Serrano Ham, Pine Nut, Lettuce & Parmesan Wraps

These wraps make a great packed lunch; they are delicious served still warm at home too.

8 small handfuls of pine nuts

8 soft flour tortillas

8 slices Serrano ham (or use prosciutto, if you prefer)

1 Romano lettuce, shredded

125 g/4¼ oz. Parmesan cheese shavings

3–4 tablespoons garlic mayonnaise

sea salt and freshly ground black pepper

MAKES 8 WRAPS

Heat a dry frying pan/skillet over high heat until hot, then add the pine nuts and cook for 3–4 minutes until lightly toasted. Remove the pine nuts from the pan and set aside.

Put the tortillas into the same pan, one at a time, for about 20 seconds each, until warm.

Lay the warm tortillas on a board or plate and put a slice of ham flat on top of each one. Put some shredded lettuce, Parmesan shavings and toasted pine nuts in the middle of each tortilla on top of the ham, dividing them evenly between each portion. Spoon a little garlic mayonnaise on the top of each and season with salt and pepper.

Fold each tortilla around the filling to make a wrap (fold up the bottom first so that the pine nuts don't drop out at the bottom). Serve immediately or let cool for a couple of minutes before wrapping in foil to take with you for a picnic or lunch.

Variation
You can use Caesar-style salad dressing or crème fraîche/sour cream instead of the mayonnaise, if you prefer.

Hot Prosciutto Parcels Stuffed with Goat's Cheese & Fresh Basil

These can be served as a canapé, in groups of three for an appetizer, or on top of a salad.

12 slices prosciutto
125 g/generous ½ cup soft goat's cheese
24 fresh basil leaves
freshly ground black pepper

MAKES 12

For each prosciutto parcel, lay a slice of prosciutto flat and put a heaped teaspoonful of the goat's cheese at one end. Place 2 basil leaves on top and sprinkle with a pinch of pepper. Fold the prosciutto over so that the goat's cheese is wrapped tightly inside. Repeat to make 12 prosciutto parcels in total.

Heat a dry frying pan/skillet (there's no need for oil if it's non-stick) or griddle pan over medium heat until hot. Put the prosciutto parcels in the hot pan and cook for about 2 minutes on each side.

Remove from the heat and let cool slightly to serve as finger food or put on top of a salad.

Variations

You can use coppa or Serrano ham instead of prosciutto, if you prefer.

Not a fan of goat's cheese? This recipe also works well with halloumi instead. Just slice the halloumi, pop it under a preheated hot grill/broiler for 4–5 minutes first until it's lightly tinged brown and then wrap the halloumi in the prosciutto slices with either the basil or fresh parsley, before cooking the parcels as above. The halloumi is a richer cheese, so you could add a squeeze of lemon juice or some balsamic vinegar on top, if you like.

Mortadella, Olive Tapenade & Rocket Sandwich

Mortadella has a tough time sometimes because it bears an unfortunate resemblance to pork luncheon meat. Please believe me when I say that's where the comparison ends; it tastes so much better and has a lovely, pure flavour and texture. This is another simple sandwich recipe combining some rich, dark flavours with the mortadella.

8 slices fresh bread of your choice
butter (at room temperature),
    for spreading
4 tablespoons Olive Tapenade
    (see page 62)
8 slices mortadella
a large handful of rocket/arugula
balsamic vinegar, to drizzle

MAKES 4 SANDWICHES

Lightly toast the slices of bread (or use them untoasted, if you prefer).

Spread butter over the toasted bread, then spread the olive tapenade over 4 of the slices. Add the slices of mortadella (2 slices per sandwich) – it's soft to bite so you won't need to shred it. Add some rocket/arugula to each and then a drizzle of balsamic vinegar.

Top each with a second piece of toasted, buttered bread to make 4 sandwiches. Serve immediately.

Serrano Ham & Aubergine Open Sandwich

I find that I'm having open sandwiches quite often these days. I think it's because I can get more on the plate, so it's just a gluttonous thing. They're also great if you're entertaining at lunchtime, if you want something a bit fancier than a plain sandwich.

8 thin (5-mm/¼-inch thick) slices aubergine/eggplant
olive oil, for brushing
4 slices fresh soda bread or crusty wholemeal/whole-wheat bread (or a base of your choice – toasted English muffins also work well)
Puttanesca Relish (see page 62), for spreading, or use a condiment of your choice
8 slices Serrano ham (or use coppa or prosciutto, if you prefer)
fresh parsley, for snipping
sea salt and freshly ground black pepper

MAKES 4

Preheat the grill/broiler to high.

Put the aubergine/eggplant slices in a single layer on a baking sheet. Brush olive oil on both sides of the slices so that they're well covered, then sprinkle with salt and pepper on both sides. Grill/broil under the preheated grill/broiler for 5 minutes on each side, turning once. Remove from the heat.

Meanwhile, lightly toast the bread base, or leave it untoasted, if you prefer.

For each open sandwich, put a good spread of the relish on a slice of bread or toast. Put 2 grilled/broiled aubergine/eggplant slices on top and then ruffle 2 slices of the Serrano ham along the top. (You can shred the ham first, if you prefer, or serve it with a knife and fork so that the ham doesn't tear off the top with the first bite.) Using kitchen scissors, snip some fresh parsley on top and add a little salt and pepper. Serve immediately.

Variation

You can add some grated Parmesan or pecorino cheese on top to make even more wonderfully rich and filling sandwiches, if you like.

Chorizo, Avocado & Poached Egg Open Sandwich

This is another lovely, light lunch option and, as with the Parma Ham and Grapefruit recipe (see page 110), an open sandwich leaves a little wriggle room for individual tastebuds, so your companions can make up their own forkfuls.

4 eggs
4 x 5-cm/2-inch lengths of chorizo sticks, cut in half lengthways
olive oil, to drizzle (or butter, if preferred)
4 slices soda bread or crusty wholemeal/whole-wheat bread, lightly toasted (or a base of your choice – toasted English muffins also work well)
2 ripe avocado pears, halved, pitted and peeled
freshly ground black pepper

MAKES 4 OPEN SANDWICHES

Poach the eggs to your liking in a pan of gently simmering water. Drain just before serving.

Meanwhile, put the chorizo slices into a dry frying pan/skillet and fry for a minute or so on either side to release the oils and to warm the chorizo through. Remove from the heat.

For each open sandwich, drizzle a little olive oil on the toasted bread (or spread with butter, if you prefer). Crush half an avocado onto it using a fork, then layer 2 chorizo slices on top of the avocado. Place a poached egg on top, scrunch some black pepper over and serve immediately.

Variation
Another option (omitting the eggs, olive oil and bread base) is to finely dice the chorizo, lightly fry it, mix it with the crushed avocados, and season with pepper. This can then be served with Wholemeal Crispbread (see page 70) or Home-baked Oatcakes (see page 70), like a meaty take on guacamole.

Bruschetta with Chorizo Strips, Grilled Red Pepper & Watercress

This is one of those appetizers or light lunches that you start politely eating with a knife and fork and are relieved when someone (usually me) picks it up in one hand and eats it like a big biscuit. It's jolly easy to make too.

4 x 5-cm/2-inch lengths of chorizo
1 red (bell) pepper, deseeded
1 teaspoon olive oil
4 small handfuls of watercress
   (or salad leaves/greens of your
   choice)
4 slices Garlic-y Bruschetta
   (see page 72)
freshly ground black pepper

SERVES 4

Preheat the grill/broiler to high.

First, slice the chorizo pieces in half lengthways to make a total of 8 halves. Set aside.

Cut the red (bell) pepper into quarters and then cut each quarter into quarters again, making them as flat as you can. Rub the olive oil all over the pepper pieces, then put them in a single layer on a baking sheet along with the halved chorizo pieces.

Pop them under the preheated grill/broiler for 5–6 minutes, until the red (bell) pepper is starting to brown on the edges and become soft. Remove from the heat.

For each serving, put a small handful of watercress on top of a slice of bruschetta and then layer 2 pieces of chorizo and 4 pieces of grilled/broiled red (bell) pepper on top. Add a good scrunch of pepper to each serving. You probably won't need salt with the chorizo, but add it if you like. Serve immediately.

COOKING WITH CHARCUTERIE

Leftover Roast Ham Omelette

The simple omelette/omelet is one of my favourite ways to use up leftover cold roast ham. Even the shredded bits left on the board are perfect for the omelette mixture.

6 eggs
a good splash of milk, about
    25 ml/1½ tablespoons
1 tablespoon freshly chopped
    parsley
a small pinch of mustard powder
a handful of leftover cold cooked
    ham, chopped or shredded
a handful of mature Cheddar
    cheese, cubed (optional)
20 g/generous 1 tablespoon butter
sea salt and freshly ground
    black pepper

SERVES 2

Crack the eggs into a bowl and beat them really well, then add the milk, parsley and mustard powder, season with salt and pepper, and mix well. Throw in the ham and cubes of Cheddar, if using.

Heat the butter in a frying pan/skillet over fairly high heat until it's fully melted and the pan is very hot. Pour in the egg mixture, pushing any away from the sides of the pan. Turn the heat right down and let the omelette/omelet cook slowly.

Once the bottom half of the omelette/omelet is solid, you can use a heatproof spatula to flip one side over. Cook until the eggs are set. Alternatively, leave the omelette/omelet flat and finish it under a hot grill/broiler.

Once the omelette/omelet is cooked, serve it immediately.

Cook's Note
If you want a slightly more filling meal, this is great served with Sweet Patatas Bravas (see page 69), as the tomato sauce is as lovely with the omelette/omelet as it is with the roasted sweet potatoes.

Asparagus & Prosciutto Gratin

This is a delightful side dish to serve when asparagus is in season. It doesn't take much effort to put together and is always a crowd-pleaser at dinner parties.

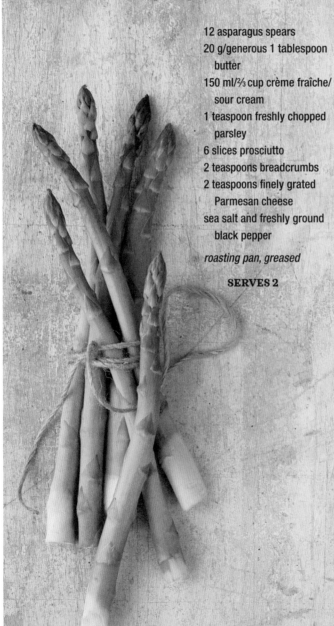

12 asparagus spears
20 g/generous 1 tablespoon
  butter
150 ml/⅔ cup crème fraîche/
  sour cream
1 teaspoon freshly chopped
  parsley
6 slices prosciutto
2 teaspoons breadcrumbs
2 teaspoons finely grated
  Parmesan cheese
sea salt and freshly ground
  black pepper

roasting pan, greased

SERVES 2

Bend each asparagus spear until it snaps, and discard the woody ends.

Steam the asparagus spears over a pan of boiling water for about 3–4 minutes, just to soften them – you don't want them fully cooked. Set aside.

Meanwhile, melt the butter in a frying pan/skillet and then stir in the crème fraîche/sour cream. Add the chopped parsley, season with salt and pepper, and remove from the heat.

Preheat the grill/broiler to medium.

Wrap a slice of prosciutto around 2 asparagus spears and lay them in the ovenproof roasting dish. Repeat with the remaining prosciutto slices and asparagus spears, laying them side by side in the dish.

Pour the melted butter and crème fraîche/sour cream mixture evenly over the top. Mix the breadcrumbs and Parmesan cheese together in a bowl and then sprinkle this over the top.

Grill/broil for 6–8 minutes until nicely browned on top, then serve immediately.

Sliced Coppa & Spring Onion Frittata

Frittata – the Italian omelette. This can also be made as a quiche if you use the pastry recipe from the tart on page 144, but it's lovely and rich with just the cheese and meat, so I prefer it as a frittata. I like to serve this with a Pinot Grigio to balance the richness.

20 g/generous 1 tablespoon butter

8–10 spring onions/scallions, sliced

6 eggs, beaten

2 tablespoons milk

a big pinch of freshly chopped parsley

1 tablespoon crème fraîche/ sour cream

60 g/2¼ oz. soft goat's cheese (or soft cheese of your choice)

100 g/3¾ oz. coppa or salami, sliced

sea salt and freshly ground black pepper

salad leaves/greens, to serve

2 lemon quarters, to serve (optional)

SERVES 2

Heat the butter in a frying pan/skillet until melted, then fry the spring onions/scallions over high heat until soft and browned. Meanwhile, mix the eggs with the milk, parsley and some salt and pepper. Pour the beaten egg mixture over the spring onions/scallions and stir once to mix well. Turn the heat down to medium and leave the egg mixture to cook (without stirring) until it starts to thicken.

Meanwhile, preheat the grill/broiler to high.

Once the bottom of the frittata starts to set in the frying pan/skillet, put the crème fraîche/sour cream on the top of the frittata in evenly spaced 'dollops'. Do the same with the pieces of goat's cheese and then with the slices of coppa, pushing the middle of the slices down slightly so the sides fold up.

Transfer the frying pan/skillet to the preheated grill/broiler and grill/broil for about 5 minutes until the top browns. Keep checking the frittata regularly to make sure it doesn't burn.

Serve immediately, sliced into wedges. Serve with a side of dressed salad leaves/greens and a lemon quarter to squeeze over the top, if you like.

Scrambled Egg, Roasted Vine Tomatoes & Proscuitto with Porcini Mushroom Purée

When you take some of the components of a traditional 'English Breakfast' and prepare it like this, you can eat it for any meal in the day, I reckon.

15 g/½ oz. dried porcini
    mushrooms
(or 25 g/1 oz. fresh porcini
    mushrooms, finely chopped)
8 tomatoes on the vine
2 tablespoons olive oil
25 g/2 tablespoons butter,
    plus 10 g/¼ oz.
1 garlic clove
1 tablespoon crème fraîche/
    sour cream
a big pinch of freshly snipped
    chives
4 eggs
50 ml/scant ¼ cup whole milk
6 slices prosciutto
sea salt and freshly ground
    black pepper

SERVES 2

Preheat the oven to 190°C (375°F) Gas 5.

First, start the porcini mushroom purée. If you're using dried porcini mushrooms, as I usually do, soak them in boiling water for about 20 minutes, then drain and finely chop.

While the mushrooms are soaking, prepare the roasted tomatoes.

Keep the tomatoes on the vine and put them in an ovenproof dish, then drizzle over the olive oil. Season with salt and pepper. Roast in the preheated oven for 20–25 minutes until they start to brown and are soft.

Meanwhile, finish making the porcini purée. Melt the 10 g/¼ oz. butter in a frying pan/skillet, then add the garlic and soaked or fresh porcini mushrooms. Mix in the crème fraîche/sour cream and stir well. Remove from the heat and keep hot. Serve with the snipped chives sprinkled on the top.

A few minutes before you are ready to serve, make the scrambled eggs. In a bowl, beat the eggs, milk and a bit of pepper together really well. Melt the remaining 25 g/2 tablespoons butter in a separate frying pan/skillet and pour in the egg mixture, stirring constantly to keep it from setting or sticking. Continue cooking and stirring, until the eggs are scrambled to your liking.

Serve the prosciutto slices as they are, or, in the pan that you used for the porcini mushroom purée, lay the slices in there and cook for just a couple of minutes on each side, turning once, so that they start to crisp and soak up some of the flavour of the mushrooms.

Serve the scrambled eggs with the porcini purée, roasted tomatoes and prosciutto slices.

Grilled Halved Chorizo
with Paprika and Parmesan Mash

This is a charcuterie version of the traditional 'sausage and mash' meal. It's richer, with the chorizo and the flavoured mash, so that's why I would recommend mixing potato mash with squash mash to lighten it. If you normally eat three sausages, you'll probably only need three halved chorizo pieces, rather than six (that means you, Roland...).

½ butternut squash, peeled, deseeded and chopped
2 baking potatoes, chopped
15–20-cm/6–8-inch length of whole chorizo, cut into 5-cm/2-inch lengths
10 g/2 teaspoons butter
3 tablespoons milk
1 teaspoon paprika
a pinch of chipotle powder
30 g/1¼ oz. Parmesan cheese, grated
sea salt and freshly ground black pepper
snipped fresh chives or parsley, to garnish

SERVES 2

Put the squash and potatoes in a saucepan, cover with cold water, bring to the boil and boil for 15–20 minutes until cooked.

Meanwhile, preheat the grill/broiler to high.

Slice the chorizo pieces lengthways in half and peel off the casing. Pop the chorizo pieces under the grill/broiler for 10 minutes, turning once. A good chorizo shouldn't shrivel too much, but just keep an eye on it. Remove from the heat.

Drain the squash and potatoes, return to the pan and mash well with the butter and milk. Add the paprika, chipotle powder and Parmesan, and season with salt and pepper. Stir well.

Serve the mash with the grilled/broiled chorizo and garnish with some snips of fresh chives or parsley on top. This dish goes well with Sweet Chilli Sticky Sweetcorn (see page 65).

Tarte au Saucisson Sec with
Caramelized Red Onion, Brie & Tarragon Pastry

This was the first recipe I tried for this book! It was a regular Tuesday evening and Roland said, 'What's for supper?' When I replied with this title, he realized that supper was going to be a lot of fun for a couple of months. He also realized that he might have to plan to go to the gym a little more too. (NB I know ours was a rather gender-stereotyped exchange about supper, but even when Roland insists on doing the cooking, it starts with a bit of fussing on my part and ends in a coup d'état, so he finds jobs elsewhere...!).

1 red onion, thinly sliced
2 tablespoons runny honey
100 g/3½ oz. butter (at room temperature)
220 g/1¾ cups plain/all-purpose flour
a big pinch of sea salt
a big pinch of dried tarragon
200 g/7 oz. Brie, sliced
7–8 slices saucisson sec (about 60 g/2¼ oz.)
100 ml/⅓ cup crème fraîche/ sour cream
freshly ground black pepper
dressed salad leaves/greens, to serve

tart pan or baking sheet, greased

SERVES 2

Preheat the oven to 180°C (350°F) Gas 4.

Put the onion in an ovenproof dish, drizzle over the honey and stir to mix. Roast in the preheated oven for 15 minutes until caramelized.

Meanwhile, to make the pastry base, rub the butter and flour together in a bowl with your fingers until crumbly, then add the salt and tarragon. Add about 1 tablespoon cold water and mix to make a dough, but don't let the mixture get too soggy. Gather the pastry into a ball, then turn it out onto a flour-dusted surface and roll out.

Use the rolling pin to help you transfer the pastry to the prepared tart pan and gently press it into the base and up the sides of the pan (or transfer the pastry to a greased baking sheet if you don't have a suitable tart pan – just make sure you fold in the edges so the topping doesn't leak out during cooking).

Prick the base of the pastry all over with a fork, then bake the pastry base on its own in the preheated oven for 5 minutes. Arrange the Brie slices over the pastry base, then sprinkle the caramelized onions over the top. Put the slices of saucisson sec over the onions, then add little blobs of crème fraîche/sour cream around the top. Add a sprinkling of pepper.

Bake in the preheated oven for a further 20–25 minutes.

Serve with dressed salad leaves/greens and an ice-cold glass of wine or cider.

Home-made Pizza

What better way to celebrate salumi than by putting it on an Italian pizza with Italian cheese? The look of the pepperoni pizza is often associated with cheap, poor-quality pizzas, but it is so different when you make it yourself and use good-quality ingredients. The ease of this recipe is that only the dough needs any preparation; the other ingredients are already prepared for you.

FOR THE BASE/CRUST

170 g/1½ cups plain/all-purpose or wholemeal/whole-wheat flour

a small pinch of fast-action/rapid-rise yeast

1 tablespoon olive oil

a pinch of sea salt

2 teaspoons caster/granulated sugar

FOR THE TOPPING

400-g/14-oz. can of tomatoes, drained and chopped

1 tablespoon tomato purée/paste

a big pinch of freshly chopped parsley

a big pinch of freshly chopped or dried oregano

about 40 g/1½ oz. Caramelized Red Onions (see page 61) (optional)

150 g/5 oz. mozzarella cheese, torn into pieces

8–10 slices salami or saucisson sec

50 g/2 oz. pecorino cheese, grated or shaved

a few fresh basil leaves

sea salt and freshly ground black pepper

a large baking sheet, greased or lined with parchment paper

MAKES 1 PIZZA

Preheat the oven to 180°C (350°F) Gas 4.

For the base/crust, put all the ingredients in a bowl, add 125 ml/½ cup water and mix together with your hands to make a dough. If the mixture feels sloppy, just add a little more flour, or add a little more water for the opposite (it shouldn't be so dry that it crumbles when you roll it). Turn the dough out onto a flour-dusted surface and knead for 5–10 minutes until smooth and elastic. The kneading is always a bit boring but just remember that you need (groan!) to do it or your base will be chewy and tough. If you have a bread maker, it will do the work for you – just follow the timing instructions for your machine.

Place the dough back in the bowl and cover with a damp tea towel/kitchen towel for about 1 hour, until risen slightly.

Transfer the dough to a flour-dusted surface and punch it down gently to release the air. Roll out the dough to a large round – we like a thin pizza base/crust but you can keep it thicker, if you prefer. Put the pizza base/crust on the prepared baking sheet and bake in the preheated oven for 10 minutes, turning over halfway through. It really helps to part-bake the base/crust on its own like this first, so that you don't have to bake it for too long with the topping on (and risk the topping burning or shrivelling up).

Meanwhile, prepare the topping. Mix the canned tomatoes, tomato purée/paste, parsley and oregano in a bowl, and season with salt and pepper.

Remove the pizza base/crust from the oven and turn it over so the softer side that was touching the baking sheet is now facing up. Spread the tomato mixture evenly over the top and then spoon over the caramelized onions, if using. Distribute the mozzarella cheese over the tomato mixture, followed by the salami slices, and finally sprinkle over the pecorino cheese. Sprinkle the basil leaves on top.

Return the pizza to the preheated oven on the middle shelf (ideally, put the pizza directly onto the oven shelf, rather than using the baking sheet, so the base/crust can continue to crisp) and bake for a further 15 minutes until the cheese has melted. Serve hot.

Pancake 'Calzones'

A savoury folded pancake with mortadella, mozzarella (or Gorgonzola) and fried Mediterranean vegetables with pesto. Not usually one to be beaten by any recipe containing meat and cheese, even my husband Roland found this recipe as a traditional calzone (made with pizza dough) a bit rich, and he had the idea of trying it as a savoury pancake, which was much less filling and also brought out the flavours of the mortadella.

FOR THE PANCAKE BATTER

40 g/⅓ cup plain/all-purpose flour
a pinch of sea salt
1 egg, beaten
50 ml/scant ¼ cup milk
20 g/generous 1 tablespoon butter

FOR THE FILLING

1 garlic clove, finely chopped
6–7 button/white mushrooms, sliced
1 courgette/zucchini, thinly sliced
1 tablespoon olive oil
4–5 sun-dried tomatoes, chopped
200-g/7-oz. can of tomatoes, drained
1 tablespoon tomato purée/paste
1 tablespoon pesto
a handful of fresh basil leaves
200 g/7 oz. mortadella, torn into pieces
200 g/7 oz. mozzarella, torn (or use Gorgonzola, crumbled, for a richer feast)
sea salt and freshly ground black pepper

MAKES 2

To make the batter, sift the flour and salt into a bowl, then whisk/beat in the egg, milk and 1 tablespoon cold water to make a smooth batter. Cover and leave in the refrigerator whilst you prepare the filling.

For the filling, fry the garlic, mushrooms and courgette/zucchini with the olive oil in a frying pan/skillet over medium heat, until brown, then add the sun-dried tomatoes, canned tomatoes, tomato purée/paste, pesto and basil leaves, season with salt and pepper, and stir until hot. Remove from the heat and keep hot.

Meanwhile, make the pancakes. Heat another frying pan/skillet over medium heat and melt half the butter. Once the butter is melted, pour half of the batter evenly into the pan, swirling it around to coat the bottom of the pan, and leave to cook.

Once the bottom is cooked, flip the pancake over, then spoon half of the vegetable mixture onto one side of the pancake. Quickly add half of the mortadella and mozzarella, then fold the pancake over and keep it over low heat for 1–2 minutes more, until the cheese has melted. Repeat with the remaining butter, batter and vegetables to make a second calzone. Serve immediately.

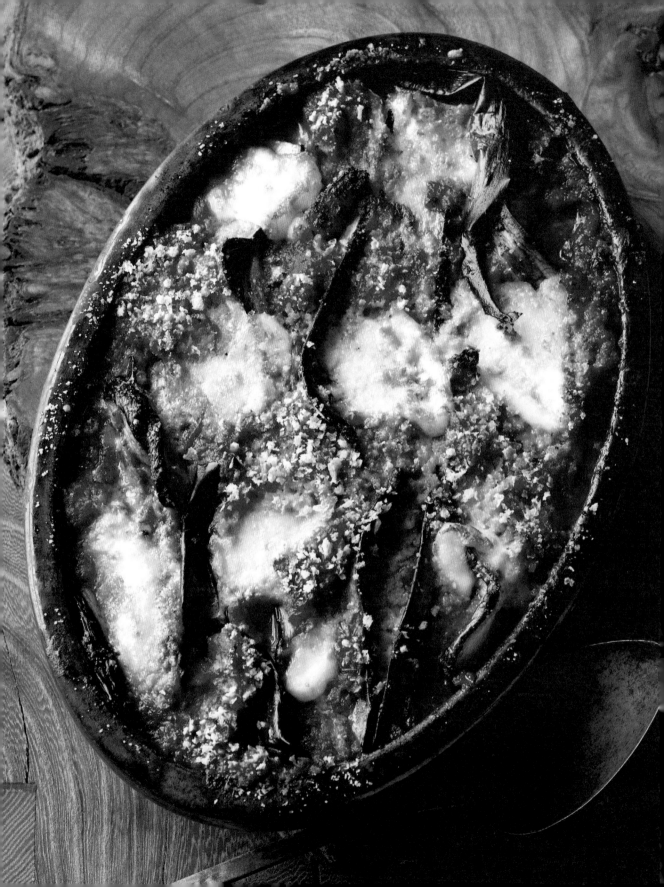

Aubergine Parmigiana

Now I know this is meant to be a vegetarian dish, but I'm incapable of leaving meat out of a recipe. I just am. If you can make the tomato sauce the day before and chill it in the refrigerator overnight, the flavour is better.

3 aubergines/eggplants, cut into
    5-mm/¼-inch slices
1 onion, finely chopped
1 garlic clove, finely chopped
100 g/3¾ oz. pancetta, diced
1 teaspoon tomato purée/paste
freshly chopped or dried oregano
1 teaspoon soft/packed brown
    sugar
a small pinch of ground nutmeg
1 tablespoon white wine vinegar
2 x 400-g/14-oz. cans of chopped
    tomatoes
10–12 fresh basil leaves
300 g/11 oz. buffalo mozzarella,
    drained
1 teaspoon finely grated Parmesan
    cheese
1 teaspoon breadcrumbs
sea salt and freshly ground
    black pepper
olive oil, for cooking

large ovenproof dish
    (about 35 x 25 cm/
    14 x 10 inches), greased

SERVES 2

Preheat the grill/broiler to high.

Rub olive oil over some foil or onto a baking sheet and set aside. Rub more olive oil over the top of each slice of aubergine/eggplant. Put a single layer of aubergine/eggplant slices on the prepared baking sheet. Grill/broil under the preheated grill/broiler for 4–5 minutes on each side and then remove to a plate. Grill/broil the remaining aubergine/eggplant slices in the same way, cooking them in batches. You can then lay the cooked slices on some paper towels to soak up some of the olive oil, if you want to. Set aside.

Meanwhile, to make the tomato sauce, fry the onion, garlic and pancetta in a frying pan/skillet with a little olive oil until they're all soft and browned. Add the tomato purée/paste, oregano, sugar and nutmeg, and season with salt and pepper. Stir for a minute. Add the vinegar and then add the canned tomatoes. Tear in the basil leaves, then reduce the heat to low and simmer for 10 minutes. Remove from the heat and let cool.

Now you are ready to assemble the dish.

Preheat the oven to 180°C (350°F) Gas 4.

Spread some of the tomato sauce over the base of the prepared ovenproof dish, then lay some of the aubergine/eggplant slices over the top to cover the sauce. Take a third of the mozzarella and tear it into little strips, then sprinkle over the aubergine/eggplant slices.

Spoon over some more tomato sauce and repeat the layer of aubergine/eggplant slices, then another third of the mozzarella. Repeat the layers for a third and final time, finishing with a last bit of tomato sauce dotted about on the top. Mix the Parmesan cheese and breadcrumbs in a bowl, then sprinkle over the top.

Bake in the preheated oven for 25 minutes. If you want to brown the top a little more, pop the dish under a preheated hot grill/broiler for 2–3 minutes so the topping browns off nicely. The mozzarella will be melted and gooey on every layer, and the sauce with the added pancetta is delicious and thick between the aubergine/eggplant slices. Serve immediately.

This is my sister's favourite dish, so I'm going to recommend a glass of sparkling rosé to go with it, because I know she loves that too!

Spaghetti Carbonara

200 g/7 oz. dried spaghetti
or linguine
50 g/3½ tablespoons butter
2 garlic cloves, finely chopped
200 g/7 oz. pancetta or streaky/
fatty bacon, cut into small cubes
2 eggs, beaten
75 g/scant ½ cup finely grated
Parmesan cheese
a big pinch of freshly chopped
parsley
1 tablespoon crème fraîche/sour
cream
sea salt and freshly ground
black pepper

SERVES 2

It's best to buy really good-quality pancetta or bacon for a really good-quality carbonara. It's such a simple dish, but it's always a popular one thanks to its perfect balance of salty pancetta and creamy eggs. It just needs plenty of black pepper, a sprinkling of fresh parsley and some grated Parmesan cheese on top to finish it off.

First, cook the spaghetti in a pan of lightly salted boiling water until it is cooked to your liking. Once the spaghetti is cooked, drain it, reserving 5-mm/¼-inch of the cooking water in the base of the pan, and keep this over low heat.

Meanwhile, melt the butter in a frying pan/skillet over medium heat and fry the garlic until soft. Add the pancetta and fry until crispy and browned. Remove from the heat and keep warm in the pan.

In a large bowl, beat the eggs and then mix in most of the Parmesan cheese, reserving just a little cheese to sprinkle on the top. Add the parsley and crème fraîche/sour cream and a good crunch of black pepper. Set aside.

Add the drained hot spaghetti to the beaten egg mixture and mix a little, then return the spaghetti and egg mixture to the pan containing the reserved pasta cooking water and stir. You don't want the egg mixture to scramble, but let it mix with the hot pasta water to create a sauce. Stir in the crispy pancetta and garlic mixture.

Serve immediately with the remaining Parmesan cheese sprinkled on top, and a crunch more pepper or a little more freshly chopped parsley, as you wish.

Mediterranean Pasta Bake
with Crispy Baked Salumi

This is a good one for entertaining because you can prepare and throw everything together earlier in the day, then all you have to do is bake the dish and add the crispy salumi in the last 10 minutes. It looks like more effort than it is as well.

FOR THE PASTA BAKE

1 tablespoon olive oil

1 red onion, finely chopped

2 garlic cloves, finely chopped

1 courgette/zucchini, chopped

1 aubergine/eggplant, chopped

1 red (bell) pepper, deseeded and chopped

8–10 button/white mushrooms, chopped

2 tablespoons tomato purée/paste

1 tablespoon pesto

2 x 400-g/7-oz. cans of chopped tomatoes

8 handfuls of dried pasta

250 ml/1 cup crème fraîche/ sour cream

200 g/7 oz. mozzarella, torn into pieces

4 Salumi Chips (see page 77)

sea salt and freshly ground black pepper

SERVES 4

For the pasta bake, heat the olive oil in a frying pan/skillet over medium heat until hot, then add the onion, garlic, courgette/zucchini, aubergine/eggplant, red (bell) pepper and mushrooms, and fry until they're all soft and browning. Add the tomato purée/paste and pesto, season with salt and pepper, and stir together for a minute, then add the canned tomatoes. Reduce the heat and simmer for 10 minutes.

Meanwhile, cook the pasta in a large pan of lightly salted boiling water for 3 minutes (it's only to soften it), then drain well and return to the pan. Add the vegetable mixture and stir well, then stir in the crème fraîche/sour cream. Taste and add more seasoning, if you like. Transfer the mixture to an ovenproof dish and spread evenly. At this point, you can cover the dish with foil and leave it for a while before baking, or cool it, then chill in the refrigerator for up to 2 days.

When you are ready to serve, preheat the oven to 180°C (350°F) Gas 4.

Dot the mozzarella over the top of the pasta mixture, then cover with foil and bake in the preheated oven for 30 minutes. After around 25 minutes, remove the aluminium foil to brown the top (alternatively, pop the pasta bake under a preheated hot grill/broiler for the last 5 minutes to brown the top).

Serve the pasta bake with the crispy salumi alongside, on top or on the side.

Chorizo, Spring Onion & Mango Noodles

I don't think there's any reason to be nervous about mixing up the geography of food; salumi can be delicious in East Asian dishes. It's a bit like this recipe, with sweetness in the mango, a kick from the chilli/chile, and then the flavours of the diced chorizo or, if you can get it, soppressata, another lovely, rich cured pork product.

1 tablespoon sesame oil
8 spring onions/scallions, chopped
1 garlic clove, finely chopped
200 g/7 oz. chorizo, diced
    (or use soppressata)
a pinch of ground ginger (or use
    grated peeled fresh root ginger)
1 small fresh red chilli/chile,
    deseeded and chopped
1 pak choi/bok choy, chopped
1 teaspoon soft/packed brown
    sugar
2 tablespoons soy sauce
a big pinch of freshly chopped
    coriander/cilantro
½ mango, peeled, stoned/pitted
    and chopped
250 g/8 oz. noodles
    (see Cook's Note)
sea salt and freshly ground
    black pepper

SERVES 2

Heat the sesame oil in a frying pan/skillet or wok and fry the spring onions/scallions and garlic over medium-high heat until soft and brown. Add the chorizo, ginger, red chilli/chile and pak choi/bok choy, and season with salt and pepper, then cook, stirring for a minute or two, until the pak choi/bok choy starts to soften. Add the sugar, soy sauce and coriander/cilantro, and stir well. Add the mango on top for the last few minutes of cooking.

Meanwhile, cook the noodles as instructed on the packet. Drain well.

Add the cooked noodles to the stir-fried mixture and toss to mix. Serve immediately, or cool, chill and eat it cold the next day.

Cook's Note
This dish is particularly good made with rice noodles, as the chorizo gives a richer flavour than is usual in this type of dish.

Chorizo & Bean Burger

I would find it impossible to compile any collection of recipes without including a beloved burger (and do a little new product development in the process!). Having always enjoyed the flavour combination of beef and pork, I love the mixture of fresh minced/ground beef with a cured pork, like chorizo.

FOR THE BURGERS
400 g/14 oz. lean minced/
    ground beef
125 g/4½ oz. chorizo, finely diced
80 g/3¼ oz. canned red kidney
    beans (drained weight), rinsed,
    drained and crushed
60 g/2¼ oz. breadcrumbs
4 teaspoons tomato purée/paste
1 teaspoon freshly chopped
    parsley
sea salt and freshly ground
    black pepper

TO SERVE
4 crusty bread rolls or toasted
    English muffins, halved
salad leaves/greens
Puttanesca Relish (see page 62),
    Sweet Chilli Sticky Sweetcorn
    (see page 65) or Caramelized
    Red Onions (see page 61)

SERVES 4
(MAKES 4 CHUNKY
175 G/6 OZ. BURGERS)

Put all the burger ingredients in a large bowl and mix together really well with your hands. Divide the mixture into 4 and then shape each portion into a burger.

To cook the burgers, fry them in a frying pan/skillet over medium heat for 12–15 minutes, turning a few times until cooked through. Alternatively, pop them on the rack in a grill/broiler pan and cook under a preheated hot grill/broiler for 6 minutes on each side until cooked through.

Serve the hot burgers in the bread rolls with some salad leaves/greens and the condiment of your choice.

Slow-cooked, Dry-rub Pork Ribs
with BBQ Sauce

The process of curing and preserving has taught us a lot about flavour. Dry rubs, for example, are short cures designed more for flavour than shelf-life, but they still follow the same process of rubbing the seasoning into the outside of meat so that it can soak up the salt and flavours. You'll need to start this the day before you want to serve it.

1 pork rack, about 5 or 6 bones
  (about 1.5 kg/3½ lbs.), trimmed
2 tablespoons sea salt
2 tablespoons dark soft/packed
  brown sugar
2 teaspoons paprika
½ teaspoon cayenne pepper
3 tablespoons brandy
Chunky BBQ Sauce, to serve
  (see page 64)

SERVES 4

Remove the fat along the top of the pork rack using a sharp knife, and set the fat aside. Mix the salt, sugar, paprika and cayenne pepper together in a bowl and then rub most of this mixture all over the joint – be sure to get in-between the trimmed bones. Place the reserved layer of fat back on top of the rack, then rub the remaining seasoning mixture over the top of that too. Wrap the joint in clingfilm/plastic wrap and leave in the refrigerator overnight or for at least 3 hours.

Preheat the oven to 200°C (400°F) Gas 6.

Unwrap the joint and put it in an ovenproof dish or roasting pan. Drizzle the brandy over the top. Roast in the preheated oven for 25–30 minutes, so the outside just begins to brown. Reduce the oven temperature down to 120°C (250°F) Gas ½. Remove the dish or pan from the oven and transfer the joint onto some foil (I recommend doubling the foil so it's stronger). Wrap the foil over the top of the joint, enclosing the meat, then return it to the dish or pan. Pour in some water around the edge so that it's about 2-cm/¾-inch high in the dish. Return to the oven and cook for a further 3 hours.

Remove from the oven. Carefully open the foil and use a fork to test the meat – put the fork into the side of the joint and twist; if the meat is still solid and doesn't shred at all, it needs longer in the oven. Return it to the oven and check again after 30 minutes. When it's ready, the joint won't fall apart at the sides, but you should be able to turn the fork and see the pork meat start to shred.

Turn the oven back up to 200°C (400°F) Gas 6.

Undo the aluminium foil and remove the layer of fat from the top of the joint (you can make crackling with this, if you like), then, with the aluminium foil still open to expose the joint, return it to the hot oven for 20 minutes until the top is crisp.

Remove from the oven. You can then slice the joint between the bones and serve it as chops or strip the meat off the bone, pull/shred it, then serve in a roll with the Chunky BBQ Sauce.

Spanish-style Paella Rice

1 tablespoon olive oil

4 shallots, finely chopped

1 garlic clove, finely chopped

100 g/3¾ oz. skinless, boneless
chicken breast or thigh meat,
diced

100 g/3¾ oz. chorizo, diced

100 g/3¾ oz. pancetta, diced

1 red (bell) pepper, deseeded
and roughly chopped

a small handful of green beans,
trimmed and roughly chopped

200 g/7 oz. shelled uncooked
seafood (such as scallops,
mussels and sliced squid)

12–14 uncooked king prawns/
jumbo shrimp, shelled and
deveined

1 small fresh red chilli/chili,
deseeded and finely chopped

1 teaspoon paprika

a pinch of chipotle powder
(optional)

50 g/½ cup frozen or fresh peas

a small handful of freshly chopped
parsley

a pinch of freshly chopped
or dried thyme

6 tablespoons white wine
(preferably dry)

500 ml/generous 2 cups hot
chicken stock

150 g/5 oz. paella rice, such
as Bomba

a small pinch of saffron strands

sea salt and freshly ground
black pepper

crème fraîche/sour cream
and 1 lemon, quartered,
to serve (optional)

SERVES 2

If I wasn't laughed at so much when I asked if 'paella' was Spanish for 'bung it all in a pan and let it go gooey', then I'd still happily believe that to be the case. Paella is so simple, so delicious (to my taste and to many like me), and it's a great way to cook with chorizo. This makes 2 generous portions.

Put the olive oil in a frying pan/skillet over medium heat and get it nice and hot, then add the shallots and garlic and cook them until browned.

Then, it's a simple process of adding everything as you go through the list. Add the chicken and cook, turning regularly, until sealed. Add the chorizo and stir for about 20 seconds, then add the pancetta and cook, stirring, until the pancetta and chorizo are becoming crisp. Add the red (bell) pepper and stir for 20 seconds, then add the green beans and cook for 20 seconds. Add the seafood and prawns/shrimp, followed by the chilli/chili and spices, and stir to coat everything. Add the peas and herbs, then add the wine and turn the heat up to bubble the wine for 2 minutes. Add the stock, rice and saffron, then season with salt and pepper.

Turn the heat right down so the mixture is just lightly bubbling and cook, stirring occasionally, for about 15–20 minutes until the rice has absorbed all the liquid and all the ingredients are cooked. You'll know if you like it a bit runny, or thicker, so just keep an eye on the consistency and be sure to taste the rice towards the end of cooking so that you know it is definitely cooked. You can always add a little more hot stock if you want the rice 'fluffier' and then just cook for a bit longer.

Once the paella is ready, serve it immediately with the crème fraîche/sour cream and lemon quarters.

TAPAS

The tradition of tapas celebrates Spanish chorizo in some delicious ways as demonstrated in these recipes. (Also see page 21 for Pan-fried Chorizo in Red Wine.)

Prosciutto & Chorizo Croquetas

50 g/3½ tablespoons butter

140 g/generous 1 cup plain/
  all-purpose flour, plus
  50 g/scant ½ cup

300 ml/1¼ cups full-fat/whole milk

50 g/2 oz. chorizo, finely chopped

4 slices prosciutto, shredded

a big pinch of freshly chopped
  parsley

a pinch of dried chilli/hot pepper
  flakes (optional)

2 eggs, beaten

75 g/generous 1 cup fresh
  breadcrumbs

sea salt and freshly ground
  black pepper

olive oil, for frying

MAKES 10

Melt the butter in a frying pan/skillet and then stir in the 140 g/ generous 1 cup flour. Cook for 2 minutes, then slowly add the milk, a little at a time, stirring constantly. Cook for a couple of minutes until thick, then mix in the chorizo, prosciutto, parsley, chilli/hot pepper flakes, if using, salt and pepper.

Remove from the heat and let cool slightly, then cover with clingfilm/plastic wrap and chill in the refrigerator for 2 hours.

Form the chilled croqueta mixture into 10 little balls or sausage shapes. Put the remaining 50 g/scant ½ cup flour in a bowl or shallow dish. Dip your hands in the flour, pick up a shaped croqueta, roll it in the flour to coat, then dip it in the beaten eggs. Finally, coat it well in breadcrumbs. Repeat with all the croquetas.

Meanwhile, heat a few centimetres/inches of olive oil in a heavy-based saucepan until hot (heat enough oil to come as high as at least half the height of the croquetas in your pan). Fry the coated croquetas in the hot oil, in batches, for about 10 minutes until they are crisp and golden all over, turning occasionally. Remove from the oil using a slotted spoon and drain on paper towels. Serve hot.

Cojunudo

125 g/4½ oz. chorizo, sliced

olive oil, for frying (optional)

4 slices pan rustico
  (or bread of your choice)

4 quail's eggs

freshly ground black pepper

freshly chopped parsley, to garnish

SERVES 4

Heat a frying pan/skillet until hot and fry the chorizo slices for 2–3 minutes, turning regularly, until they have browned on both sides. Add a drop or two of olive oil to the pan if the chorizo is sticking. Transfer the chorizo slices from the pan to a plate and set aside.

Fry the slices of bread in the same pan, on both sides, to soak up the chorizo oils, then transfer to serving plates and set aside.

Crack the quail's eggs into the pan and fry until cooked to your liking. Serve the eggs and chorizo slices on top of the slices of fried bread. Season with pepper, garnish with parsley and serve.

Crisp Fried Monkfish
with Pancetta & Capers

This recipe is easy but it needs to be made just before serving, so it's not ideal for a dinner party as it will tie you up in the kitchen – even though the smells wafting from there will whet their appetites marvellously. It does look jolly snazzy though, so be sure to brag about it with a photo.

300 g/10 oz. monkfish fillets,
   sliced into strips
30 g/¼ cup plain/all-purpose flour
2 eggs, beaten
30 g/1½ cup fresh breadcrumbs
2 tablespoons olive oil
200 g/7 oz cubed pancetta
2 tablespoons small capers,
   drained
freshly grated zest of ½ lemon
1 teaspoon freshly chopped
   parsley
½ lemon, cut into quarters
2 Salumi Chips (see page 77)
   (optional)
sea salt and freshly ground
   black pepper
Asparagus and Prosciutto Gratin
   (see page 136), to serve

SERVES 2

Roll the strips of monkfish in the flour to coat all over, then dip each strip into the beaten eggs and finally coat with breadcrumbs. Reserve any leftover breadcrumbs.

Heat the olive oil in a large frying pan/skillet over medium heat. Add the pancetta and fry until crisp, then remove from the pan and set aside. Place the coated fish strips into the pan and cook for 6–7 minutes without turning, then turn them carefully and fry for a further 6–7 minutes on the other side, until crisp and cooked through. While they're frying, sprinkle the capers, lemon zest and parsley over the top so that they fry with the monkfish and pick up the oil and flavours in the pan. You can sprinkle any leftover breadcrumbs over at this stage too, if you like, so that they add a bit of crunch to the capers. Add the pancetta back into the pan when the fish is almost cooked.

Once the fish strips are cooked and crisp, remove from the heat. Serve on plates with the capers and pancetta from the pan, and some lemon wedges on the side. Serve with the Asparagus and Prosciutto Gratin. Top each portion with a baked salumi chip, if you like – either by placing them on the top or crunching them into little shards to sprinkle over the top.

Cook's Note

This is delicious served with a home-made sweet chilli sauce. Heat 40 g/3 tablespoons butter in a frying pan/skillet until melted, add 2 finely chopped deseeded chillies/chiles, stir well then add 2 tablespoons white wine vinegar and 6 tablespoons demerara/raw sugar, stirring together well. Let the mixture boil and start to thicken, then slowly add 100 ml/⅓ cup water, stirring well. Remove from the heat and let cool, either in the refrigerator or by lowering the pan into a sinkful of cold water to cool the sauce quickly.

Chicken Breast Wrapped in Prosciutto with Griddled Chicory

This makes an impressive dinner party dish and works brilliantly with Chorizo and Red Cabbage Salad (see page 120).

1 tablespoon red wine vinegar

1 tablespoon olive oil, plus extra for griddling

1 teaspoon soft/packed brown sugar

1 garlic clove, finely chopped

a big pinch of freshly chopped parsley

a pinch each of sea salt and freshly ground black pepper

2 skinless, boneless chicken breasts

4 slices prosciutto

1 chicory/Belgian endive, halved

1 teaspoon paprika

Chorizo and Red Cabbage Salad, to serve (see page 120)

SERVES 2

Put the vinegar, olive oil, sugar, garlic, parsley and salt and pepper in a bowl and mix together, then rub this mixture into the chicken breasts. Wrap the chicken in clingfilm/plastic wrap and leave in the refrigerator for at least 1 hour.

Remove from the refrigerator, then wrap each chicken breast in 2 slices of prosciutto.

Heat a ridged stove-top griddle/grill pan over high heat with a drop more olive oil added to the pan, then add the prosciutto-wrapped chicken breasts to the hot pan and cook for 6–7 minutes. Place the chicory/Belgian endive halves, flat-sides down, next to the chicken in the same pan. Turn the wrapped breasts and leave to cook on the other side until cooked through. Sprinkle the paprika over the top of the wrapped breasts and the chicory/Belgian endive.

Turn the wrapped breasts again before the end of the cooking time and you should have the nice brown griddle lines across the prosciutto. Turn the chicory/Belgian endive halves over near the end of cooking time, just to soften the outside, but they're happy staying face-down for most of the cooking time to get the nice crunchy griddle lines across them as well.

Serve with Chorizo and Red Cabbage Salad.

Scallop, Chorizo, Chilli & Quinoa Stew with Herby Dumplings

So many cured meats come from warm southern European plains where there's a sea breeze and sunshine on the roofs... However, this is a stew recipe that's perfect for when it's chilly outside and you need some central heating for the tummy. The chorizo and the chilli/chile provide the most amazing warmth with their flavour.

FOR THE STEW

20 g/generous 1 tablespoon butter
1 red onion, diced
1 garlic clove, chopped
1 red (bell) pepper, deseeded and diced
2 celery stalks, chopped
100 g/3¾ oz. chorizo, diced
1 small fresh red chilli/chile, deseeded and finely chopped
1 teaspoon paprika
30 g/scant ⅓ cup plain/all-purpose flour
500 ml/generous 2 cups chicken stock
100 g/3¾ oz. quinoa or pearl barley
200 g/7 oz. shelled scallops
sea salt and freshly ground black pepper

FOR THE HERBY DUMPLINGS (OPTIONAL)

50 g/⅓ cup shredded suet
100 g/¾ cup self-raising/ self-rising flour
a pinch of dried thyme
a pinch of dried rosemary

a baking sheet, greased

SERVES 2

For the stew, melt the butter in a frying pan/skillet, then fry the onion and garlic over low heat for 10 minutes until softened. Add the red (bell) pepper and celery, and fry until the vegetables soften. Add the chorizo, red chilli/chile and paprika, and season with salt and pepper, then stir to mix. Sprinkle the flour over the top and stir for just a minute before adding the chicken stock. Stir in the quinoa.

Bring to a simmer and simmer for 35 minutes, stirring occasionally, then add the scallops. Cook for a further 10 minutes (or 15 minutes if the scallops are frozen), until the scallops are cooked.

If you would like to make the herby dumplings, start making them as soon as the stew begins simmering.

Preheat the oven to 180°C (350°F) Gas 4.

Put all the dumpling ingredients in a bowl and stir to mix, then gradually add 50–100 ml/scant ¼–⅓ cup cold water, a little at a time, and keep mixing with your hands until the mixture comes together in a solid ball. Don't make the mixture too wet, otherwise the dumplings will be soggy.

Divide and roll the mixture into round dumplings and put them onto the prepared baking sheet. Bake in the preheated oven for 15 minutes, then add them to the stew for the last 25 minutes of cooking time. Serve hot.

Smoked Sausage Casserole

A really good-quality smoked sausage is divine. Beware of the cheaper alternatives; they're only exploiting the tradition of mixing the meat with lots of lovely herbs and seasoning and adding the smoked flavour. I'd still recommend looking at the ingredients and the traceability before buying one. This is a recipe to make a rich, warming casserole using smoked sausage – it's easy to make and it freezes well too.

20 g/generous 1 tablespoon butter
1 red onion, chopped
1 garlic clove, chopped
1 red (bell) pepper, deseeded
    and chopped
200 g/7 oz. mushrooms, halved
    (such as button/white or
    chestnut mushrooms)
5 tablespoons red wine
20 g/¾ oz. plain/all-purpose flour
400 ml/1⅔ cups chicken stock
1 bay leaf
a sprig of fresh thyme
200 g/7 oz. smoked sausage,
    chopped
sea salt and freshly ground
    black pepper

SERVES 2

Melt the butter in a heavy-based saucepan over medium heat, add the onion and garlic and fry for about 5 minutes until softened. Add the red (bell) pepper and mushrooms and cook, stirring, until they soften. Pour in the red wine and let that reduce a little, then sprinkle the flour over the top and stir for a minute or so to mix. Pour over the chicken stock and stir well. Add the herbs and smoked sausage, and season with salt and pepper.

Bring to the boil, then reduce the heat to low. Cover and simmer for 1½ hours. For a thicker casserole, leave the casserole cooking for 2 hours.

Discard the bay leaf and thyme stalk before serving. Serve with mashed potato and a glass of German beer.

Cook's Note
This casserole freezes well for up to 3 months. Defrost thoroughly and then bring gently to the boil before serving – top up the seasoning a bit if you need to as well.

Index

Recipe & Photo Credits

PHOTOGRAPHY CREDITS

Ian Wallace
*Front cover and pages
10–11, 12, 16–53, 121,
140 and 152.*

Steve Painter
All other pages with the
exception of the following:

Claire Winfield
*Pages 94, 117, 126
and 172.*

Mowie Kay
Pages 15, 90 and 109.

Kate Whitaker
Pages 110, 124 and 129.

Helen Cathcart
Pages 81 and 120.

David Munns
Pages 98 and 118.

William Reavell
Pages 77 and 82.

Tara Fisher
Page 38.

Christopher Scholey
Page 136

RECIPE CREDITS

All recipes by Miranda
Ballard with exception
of *Pages 10–53, 5 (top)
and 64* by Louise Pickford

Acknowledgements

Thank you to the team at Ryland, Peters &
Small for all the incredible work that goes into
making their beautiful books. To Julia Charles
especially for the guidance and giggles, and
to Toni Kay for the wonderful design.

Thank you to Trealy Farm, Packington Pork,
JF Edwards and all the farmers and producers
for giving us the best ingredients to work with.

To Louise Pickford for being able to make
everything even more delicious, it has been
a total pleasure to produce this book with you,
and to Ian Wallace for shooting the boards
so beautifully.

And to Ro for being my chief recipe taster
and my most beloved version of 'husbandry'.

Miranda 2023